# Entrepreneurialism and Tourism in Contemporary Vietnam

# Entrepreneurialism and Tourism in Contemporary Vietnam

Jamie Gillen

LEXINGTON BOOKS
Lanham • Boulder • New York • London

Published by Lexington Books
An imprint of The Rowman & Littlefield Publishing Group, Inc.
4501 Forbes Boulevard, Suite 200, Lanham, Maryland 20706
www.rowman.com

Unit A, Whitacre Mews, 26-34 Stannary Street, London SE11 4AB

British Library Cataloguing in Publication Information Available

**Library of Congress Cataloging-in-Publication Data**
Names: Gillen, Jamie, 1977- author.
Title: Entrepreneurialism and tourism in contemporary Vietnam / Jamie Gillen.
Description: Lanham : Lexington Books, [2016] | Includes bibliographical references and index.
Identifiers: LCCN 22015047495| ISBN 9780739173305 (cloth : alk. paper) | ISBN 9780739173312
    (electronic)
Subjects: LCSH: Tourism--Vietnam. | Entrepreneurship--Vietnam.
Classification: LCC G155.V5 G55 2016 | DDC 338.4/791597--dc23 LC record available at http://
    lccn.loc.gov/2015047495

∞™ The paper used in this publication meets the minimum requirements of American
National Standard for Information Sciences Permanence of Paper for Printed Library
Materials, ANSI/NISO Z39.48-1992.

Printed in the United States of America

# Contents

# Note on Usage of Vietnamese Diacritics

Vietnamese is a tonal language written in a Roman script. I have chosen to maintain the diacritic/tonal marks for all Vietnamese words and Vietnamese names. On the other hand, and in order to "universalize" place names for non-Vietnamese language readers, I have removed them when referring to place names in Vietnam.

# Acknowledgements

This book is the result of fieldwork conducted in Ho Chi Minh City, Vietnam, over a period of about five years, from 2002–2007, with some short follow-up visits in 2012. Thank you to the funding organizations that supported my language training and research during those years: the U.S. Fulbright Scholar Program (U.S. Department of State), the Foreign Language and Area Studies Program (FLAS, U.S. Department of Education), the University of Colorado, and the National University of Singapore. Special acknowledgement is extended to the members of the Fulbright office in Hanoi who have been consistent supporters. Gratitude is extended to my many mentors over the years, and specifically my PhD committee members (Tim Oakes, Herbert Covert, Susan Clarke, Rachel Silvey, Lynn Staeheli, and Gary Gaile (honorary)) for their support and critical feedback. Special thanks to Bert and Tim for going above and beyond for me over the years.

There are too many friends and colleagues who have stood with me while writing and thinking about this monograph, so I will simply thank them by listing my residences as a way to thank them for their love and support in these places: Oakton, Blacksburg, Charlottesville, Alexandria, Lexington, Boulder, Ho Chi Minh City, Oxford, Auburn, and Singapore. My life is immeasurably brightened by the time I've spent in these places with friends.

In particular, thank you to my respondents and friends in Ho Chi Minh City. I've been given so much, and learned so much, in my time with you.

I carry the experiences in this book with my mom Ann and brother Danny. You've given me the confidence, enthusiasm, space, and love to pursue my interest in Vietnam. My appreciation and love for you both is infinite.

Chapter 3 is an expansion of an article previously published in the journal *Political Geography* (Elsevier, 2011, 272–281). Parts of chapter 4 were published in a previous article in the journal *Urban Geography* (Taylor & Francis, 2010, 31/1 (90–113)). Parts of chapter 6 come from a chapter I published previously in an edited book entitled *Asia on Tour* (2009, London: Routledge). Thanks to these publishers for the opportunity to reprint some of this material.

# ONE

## Introduction

### ENTREPRENEURIALISM AND TOURISM IN CONTEMPORARY VIETNAM

Walk anywhere in Ho Chi Minh City (formerly and colloquially still known as Saigon), Vietnam, and you are likely to be overwhelmed with a sense of entrepreneurial spirit pervading the city's sellers. There are stalls small and large in markets across the city selling all manner of goods and services. Stall employees by turns bark encouraging invitations to "have a look" at their products and stare uninterestedly into space as they struggle to make it through another extended work shift. There are gleaming new malls replete with top international fashion and entertainment brands. In these spaces Vietnamese workers use impeccable English, Vietnamese, Japanese, Chinese, Korean, and Russian (to name but a few) to explain and share their offerings. The city is perhaps most well-known for its petty traders, however: these informal sellers roam the streets of the city—most without the requisite permits and licenses—and sell everything from shoe shines to dried cuttlefish for the Western equivalent of a couple of coins. Lurking over these traders sit gleaming office towers, mixed-use development projects, and high-rise apartment complexes that would not look out of place in Singapore. Here multinational company branch offices operate alongside prominent Vietnamese companies. Behind these walls English and Vietnamese languages intermix in the professional environment and spill into restaurants after work. Competition over the consumer dollar, like in the markets and in the streets, is ferocious. While there are significant differences between these workers, what ties them together is an overarching sense of economic possibility coupled with a sociability and a gregariousness that is not easily replicated in other places in the world.

1

This book draws attention to the ways in which the Vietnamese tourism industry shapes and is shaped by entrepreneurial actors, firms, and the state as they chase financial success. In an era in which the market reform policies initiated by the Communist Party of Vietnam (the state) in the late 1980s have reached their maturity, an examination of a neglected yet powerful segment of the Vietnamese entrepreneurial economy can shed light on the changing nature of transitional economies, state-society relations, and postsocialist governance in the non-Western world. This book uses a cultural economy framework drawn from geography, cultural studies, entrepreneurship, tourism, and Vietnamese studies alongside interviews and textual analysis of players, documents, and policies in the Vietnamese tourism industry to develop a critical framework for studying entrepreneurship in Vietnam today.

Entrepreneurialism is a useful framework for the examination of the changing face of the Vietnamese economy for several reasons. Entrepreneurship entails the acceptance of financial and "extra-economic" (Amin and Thrift 2007, 2004) risk: significant monetary losses may result from a failed business project and the interpersonal, kinship, and cultural relations between business partners may incur a similar breakdown if a project fails (Kim 2008, Yeung 2009). Successes of a variety of sorts are enjoyed if a project is successful. Because the tourism industry has lower startup costs than creating a traditional brick and mortar business, high profit margins are possible in a rapidly developing country like Vietnam (Cohen and Cohen 2012, Scheyvens 2011, Hall 2008, Hall and Page 2011). However, entrepreneurial activities are temperamental and trace (and sometimes precede) the ups and downs of the market (Silverman 2012, Gibson 2009, Tao and Wall 2009), changing gender and kinship norms (Turner 2012, Leshkowich 2011), and transforming rural-urban mobilities (Agergaard and Vu 2012, Nguyen, et al. 2012). Knowledge sharing, collaboration, reciprocity, and the role of hometown, locality, and kinship in economic relationships are among many cultural or extra-economic characteristics of entrepreneurialism yet are rarely documented in the existing literature and are thus often ill-defined and poorly understood. This vital underbelly of entrepreneurial relations is a crucial component of the manuscript. Entrepreneurialism is disposed to change through the introduction of innovative inputs, like the creation of market niches (such as new tourism routes, tourist sites, and ancillary businesses); the recalibration of Vietnamese memory sites as objects of tourist consumption; and the assignment of stereotypes to "inside" Vietnamese and "outside" foreign tourists in order to maintain Vietnamese identity categories. These are the subjects of some of the empirical chapters of this book.

While locally based entrepreneurial endeavors are a critical means of assessing the postsocialist economic landscape, there is a second account of entrepreneurship that is made meaningful by the state. As the sole political unit of the Vietnamese government, the state is in a position to establish itself as the regulator and primary competitor in the Vietnamese economy because it sees itself as the largest and most important market force in the country. The state's type of entrepreneurship—evaluated through its expression of Vietnamese national culture—is a valuable arm to exercise political power over Vietnam and is the centerpiece of chapter 3. Thus, the state's relationship to entrepreneurialism and its role in shaping local, non-state entrepreneurial activities is also threaded throughout the book. It is the tension between competing and complementary visions and practices of entrepreneurship—between local, fluid uses and the state's ideological construction of a fixed and irreducible entrepreneurial spirit—that forms the backbone of the manuscript. The book's primary research question is: what kinds of discursive entrepreneurial policies and material entrepreneurial activities do private actors, firms, and the state equip themselves with in order to compete in today's marketplace? The literature to date largely takes a top-down analytic approach to the changes to economic reform (and its cultural variations) in countries like Vietnam, China, and the former Soviet bloc countries (although see Truitt 2013, Harms 2011, Gainsborough 2010, and Nguyễn-võ 2008 for recent manuscript length reappraisals of state-society relations in Vietnam from the "ground up") without acknowledging the entrepreneurial connections and contestations between local actors and the state, an important driver to both parties' economic and political endeavors.

The two major aims of the book are: (1) an advancement of the "entrepreneurial" model of political governance that focuses on cultural and extra-economic forces, (2) the interplay and divergence of entrepreneurialism scripted by Vietnam's private tourism industry and the official ideological claims on entrepreneurialism in the absence of a transparent, "free market" playing field. I summarize each of these objectives after an introduction of Vietnam and the book's research field site, Ho Chi Minh City.

## VIETNAM AND HO CHI MINH CITY: INVESTIGATING A PRIMATE CITY IN ONE OF THE WORLD'S FASTEST GROWING ECONOMIES

The ruling state comfortably groups Vietnam among fellow postsocialist countries, including China, Russia, Cuba, and Poland (Schwenkel 2014, Zhang 2012, Oakes 2012, Chio 2011, McGee 2009, Beresford 2008, Reid-Henry 2007, Smith and Stenning 2006). Postsocialist countries are broadly defined as states that historically followed a Soviet-style command economy system and are now engaged in nationwide transitions to capitalism. This transition on the part of former-socialist economies is often understood to be a natural occurrence in the current era of globalization, one which is characterized by neoliberal policies, an increased homogeneity in market economy-based forms around the world, and the free market's ability to touch every "nook and cranny" of everyday life through its mechanisms (Schwenkel and Leshkowich 2012, Springer 2009a, 2009b, Harvey 2006).

In 1986 the state ostensibly followed the lead of former socialist countries like China and the Soviet Union and announced what the Vietnamese government called "đổi mới" ("open door" or "new change") policy reforms with an eye toward integration into the global economy. By 1985 Vietnam had completed a decade of national reunification, but the anniversary was hardly a cause for celebration. Vietnam was mired in deep-seated poverty and a corresponding feeling of despondency had firmly settled into the population. In light of these social and political problems, the government announced a broad set of policies to increase productivity, accept foreign investment, and (at the same time) retain a socialist foundation. The central tenets of the policy package, to be instituted purposefully and over time, are the decollectivization of agricultural collectives, the deregulation of state-owned enterprises (SOEs) in favor of transparent competition among private companies, and the "opening up" of the country's borders to outside investment. The latter point corresponds directly to the Vietnamese government's desire to extend its markets into the global economy, taking advantage of Vietnam's inexpensive, highly educated workforce to better the economic lives of its citizens.

The focus of Vietnam's đổi mới package is "market socialism," a phrase coined by the state. This idiom, and its repetitive use, suggests that the government continues to embrace its socialist moniker and eschews a "one-size-fits-all" economic model of globalization favored by Western leaders. The "market socialist" system is an economic paradox: the prices of goods are controlled by an unregulated *market* while socialism suggests that property and wealth are controlled by the Vietnamese *people*. This phrase is an effort to signal its direction over Vietnamese society through the đổi mới policies and to sustain its authority over the country's societal and economic affairs. When read in statistical terms, the thirty years of đổi mới policies have been remarkably successful for the national economy. Kim observes that "Vietnam has transitioned from being one of the poorest developing countries to the second fastest growing country in the world. Such cases are rare in international development, especially ones that happen so quickly" (2008: 3). She follows the World Bank's commentary by adding that Vietnam's former World Bank director, Klaus Rohland, has stated that "There's probably no other country in the world that, over the last fifteen years, has moved its development so far and so fast" (*ibid.*: 4). Moreover former World Bank president Robert Zoellick, who visited Vietnam in one of his first tours in office, has said that "Vietnam has the potential to be one of the great success stories in development" (cited in Kim 2008: 4). Data on Vietnam's success is not only strong economically. Societal and quality of life measures such as health, gender equality, and education have risen dramatically since the onset of the reform era as well. Vietnam is, with China and India, widely acknowledged to be one of Asia's development "stars."

However, with all of its free market spoils after integrating into the global economy, Vietnam's government wishes to maintain its legacy of oversight over the direction of the national economy (Gainsborough 2010). This oversight is largely driven by identifying problems and prospects associated with individualism and entrepreneurialism. According to the government, the meticulousness and hierarchical oversight of the implementation of the economic đổi mới policies are nearly as critical to the presentation of the successes of đổi mới as its actual contents (Fforde and De Vylder 1996). Far from borrowing from a global capitalist model, the government seeks to put into place a capitalist-friendly environment built on entrepreneurialism, which is state controlled and directed. Vietnam's economic and social transformations, in other words, should be conditioned by Vietnamese norms and values defined as appropriately "entrepreneurial" by the ruling authorities. A "market socialist economy" is a slogan aimed at orienting the Vietnamese economy to the government's leadership and to remind observers that the economy is built on the state's sense of a national entrepreneurial direction. And although concrete and transparent statistics are difficult to access, it is understood that the state controls the majority of the national economy through state-owned enterprise, joint ventures with private companies, and pseudo-private companies that are in fact under the direction of government officials (Gainsborough 2010). In the government's case, because the state owns and operates so many businesses throughout the country it has only recently experienced competition from foreign corporations and upstart Vietnamese companies. Thus, this book aligns with Gainsborough who

> is not very sympathetic towards ideas of state retreat (although it is open to state change) . . . (state retreat implies) the unmediated advance of neoliberalism or liberal democracy (even if not now but "some time in the future," as is often implied), or positions which emphasize the very great power of external forces in relations to something more indigenous. (2010: 2)

I argue that continuing to control the national market in an era where foreign investment and private entrepreneurship has exponentially increased is one of the state's goals and it is accomplished through heightened concern with and attention to appropriate forms of entrepreneurialism, illustrated as they are by the conceptualization and maintenance of Vietnamese culture. As such, this book takes a skeptical approach to the inception of neoliberalism in contemporary Vietnam.

This, however, does not mean that the state's part of the economic "pie" results in less for the private sector. This book disputes a "zero-sum" economic game for the state and society in Vietnam and instead advances the notion that Vietnam's reform era has been largely beneficial for the state and the non-state (private) sector. In this way the book aims to counter a "strong state" model of economic governance over Vietnamese society because of the fluidity between "state" and "society" and also—when such divisions are necessary to make—as a negotiable and rapidly transforming relationship between them. For the state a new national economy has existed since the introduction of the đổi mới policies and the policies have fostered economic opportunities for many Vietnamese citizens unaffiliated with the current regime as well as for members of the government. The opening of the country to foreign investment has meant a diversification of the government's economic portfolio, but the new economy also poses a threat to the state's economic and political leadership, primarily because the rules and codes prefiguring a homogenous economic model that "globalizes" the world is centered on representative democracy and neoliberal economic markets that often reduces the role of the state. The government's vision of entrepreneurialism has been transformed in order to mask its rent-seeking and its desire to use forms of entrepreneurialism to maintain national power.

Designing and controlling entrepreneurialism in Ho Chi Minh City, a city with mammoth economic output and the majority of Vietnam's foreign-owned businesses, would seem a daunting task for officials. Truitt's argument that "today Ho Chi Minh City is the commercial center of Vietnam, but it is still enmeshed within the institutional apparatus of the territorial state. Not only does the city attract massive flows of foreign direct investment, but it is a major contributor to national gross domestic product and the government's fiscal base" (2013: 9) resonates with the way in which the city is treated in this book (Figure 1.1). Ho Chi Minh City's gains have arisen in large part out of the private (and foreign) capital and transnational companies that have set up shop in the city.

As a further context for the book, I wish to show that the state accepts the economic supremacy of Ho Chi Minh City but uses it (and Vietnamese cities in general) as examples of the cultural pitfalls of an unbridled free market (Hoang 2011, Nguyễn-võ 2008, P. Taylor 2003, 2001). For example, in one of the government's cultural documents in which Vietnamese culture is clarified, leaders invoke this charge to Vietnamese people, "(We) encourage the cities . . . to increase their investment in culture" (Lê 2005: 17). In this passage the state seems to believe that urban economic growth is competing (and winning) with Vietnamese culture for currency in cities like Ho Chi Minh City. Buttressing unbridled free markets with national cultural inputs would seem to rectify the imbalance between culture and economy in the city. Yet Ho Chi Minh City's historically contrarian position within the country further magnifies today's cultural and economic issues. Ho Chi Minh City has long been understood as a hotbed of dissenting views, some of which materialized into unique relig-

**Figure 1.1.   Map of Vietnam. Created by Lee Li Kheng.**

ions (such as the Hòa Hảo and the Cao Đài religions), and others in the form of political alignment with French and American colonialists (see Peycam 2012, McHale 2004).

   In a country whose leadership takes pride in its rural backbone, the government states that one-third of the Vietnamese population are now urban dwellers (Gainsborough 2010: 15), a consequence of the reform policies that stressed increased private market accessibility and the decentralization of governance from the capital to individual city managers in places like Ho Chi Minh City, Hanoi, Danang, Haiphong, and Can Tho. And Ho Chi Minh City, as the country's primate city, is a unique city among these. For Gainsborough,

> Ho Chi Minh City stands out from the rest of Vietnam in a variety of ways. It is Vietnam's largest city. It is the country's economic powerhouse. It is Vietnam's richest city. During the reform era, Ho Chi Minh City has attracted more foreign direct investment than any other province or municipality. Compared with Hanoi, Ho Chi Minh City also feels different. Part of this has to do with climatic differences, but cultural differences—not influenced by climate—are real enough. This is evident in the perceptions that Vietnamese commonly have of themselves—and readily share with outsiders. Southerners typically described themselves as more carefree, less risk-averse, more outspoken, and less formal than their northern counterparts. (*ibid.*: 25)

Thus, there is a political logic concerned with Ho Chi Minh City's erasure of a vaguely defined Vietnamese "spirit" through its rabid consumerism and rampant entrepreneurialism (Harms 2013, Hoang 2011, Kim 2009, Nguyễn-võ 2008). From the state's standpoint, however, this book argues that this approach is a discourse used to legitimate the government's concern for Ho Chi Minh City's entrepreneurial strength, where competition from private industry over state economic interests is at its most fierce. Ho Chi Minh City is seemingly a city free of Vietnam's demands to maintain "market socialism" and is therefore a lynchpin for the tensions between the state and Vietnamese society that I intend to capture in an appraisal of the Vietnamese economy in this manuscript.

## CONCEPTUAL FRAMEWORK

### Rethinking the entrepreneurial model of political governance

An overview of the study site provides the background for the two major theoretical pulses of the book: (1) an assessment of the undertheorization of cultural inputs in an entrepreneurial model of political governance and the consequences of this gap on the model itself, (2) the expedient aspects of two competing claims on entrepreneurship by players in the Ho Chi Minh City tourism industry and the local branch of the state. A critique of Harvey's (1989) entrepreneurial modeling of urban governance, which has been extended into geographic analyses of entrepreneurialism in cities (Harvey 2005, Wu 2002, and Hall and Hubbard 1998) is countered by a hybrid cultural-economic alternative introduced in geography by Amin and Thrift 2007, 2004). This serves as the primary theoretical driver to my empirical findings.

The entrepreneurial city model is an approach to analyze cities in eras of late capitalism and is perhaps most famously attributed to Harvey's seminal paper in the late 1980s. "Urban governments acting more like private businesses than managerial institutions" is often the concise definition given to entrepreneurial cities (Harvey 1989). Entrepreneurial governance, like other theorizations of cities after deindustrialization in political science and sociology (Savitch and Kantor 2004, Hall and Hubbard 1996, Judd and Ready 1986, Peterson 1981), is characterized by regime-building on the part of a variety of public officials and private actors and their interests in local urban development. In general entrepreneurial cities formed following the withdrawal of state financing to urban areas in the 1970s and 1980s, forcing Western cities to fend for themselves through highly speculative, risky projects. Other urban scholars date aspects of urban entrepreneurship much earlier (see Schumpeter 1934), arguing that urban boosterist strategies for development in the late 1800s and early 1900s are similar to today's entrepreneurial strategies because they both rely heavily on discourses of innovation shot through representations and symbols of cultural significance (Jessop and Sum 2000).

Perhaps most importantly to the entrepreneurial city model is that it has served as a template for neoliberal models of national governance outlined by Harvey and others (see Peck, Theodore, and Brenner 2010; Springer 2010; Leitner, Peck, and Sheppard 2007). The retraction of the state from social welfare programs in cities has been a precursor to the retraction of the state from social services across nations. Now, according to neoliberal ideologies, the impetus for economic support from the state is limited to allowing risky, private programs to take root (with cheerleading and marketing from the state), which by largely ignoring social services disregards basic human needs such as health care, housing, education, and the right to work. In most of the existing literature it is presumed that Asian countries have followed suit from Western countries and are seeing varying levels of national wealth increases but have been inevitably hurt by one of neoliberalism's principal tenets: the concentration of capital and the means of production in the hands of the elite (e.g., Kim and Wainwright 2010, Harvey 2005). These models have made important contributions to geography and the social sciences in general but do not, as I show below, mirror the path of the Vietnamese economy since the onset of the nation's market reform policies.

What is most critical for the purposes of this manuscript's critique is that entrepreneurial and neoliberal models deem cultural strategies to be the outcomes of shifts in the economy. Under these models, there is no constitutive relationship between the economy and culture in the production of places. Rather, culture and economy exist in separate conceptual and practical spheres with the (capitalist) economy serving as both the

foundation for localized exchanges and the catalyst to place-based transformations in general. "Economic" models of entrepreneurialism tend to
neglect the processes by which entrepreneurs identify culture's appeal in
situ and iron out its usefulness in attracting the consumer dollar. Although Harvey developed the model with reference to urban development, he has more recently presented similar findings among national
regimes, including in the postsocialist, non-Western world of China (Harvey 2005). His findings have also been tested and reinforced by other
scholars working in Asia (He and Wu 2009).

*Cultural-Economy*

My study critiques hard economic approaches to social changes in
Vietnam and instead begins with the position that culture and economy
cannot be divorced conceptually or in practice at any scale of analysis;
they are best understood as a "hybrid entanglement," following Amin
and Thrift's work (2007, 2004). This work has two overarching goals: to
connect two historically separate terms and rethink the economy through
a cultural-economy perspective (Amin and Thrift 2007: 150). While others
analyze the contemporary relationships between culture and economy in
geography (Barnes 2005, 2003, Allen 2002), Amin and Thrift position their
analysis as a correction to decades of supposed rational economic theorizing within the economic academic community. They argue that culture
has long been viewed in economic theorizing as either an outcome of
economic processes (such as in Harvey's work), or as a variable or condition that affects the architecture of economic production, consumption,
circulation, and distribution. To dismiss culture as an offshoot or variable
to the economy provides advantages to the economy as the primary
foundation and driver of social life. In other words (and following these
ideas), this work argues against rendering the economy as something
more concrete or pivotal than culture.

A cultural-economic approach begins with the triadic relationship between actors (including firms and political parties), cultural performances and knowledges, and economic transactions. Cities such as Ho
Chi Minh City include actors with sustained interests in performing specific perspectives of culture for economic benefit. These forces, or "impulses" (Amin and Thrift 2007) are brought to the forefront of economic
life in cities through everyday relations between actors, and the unique
dimensions of these cultural-economic impulses do something to form
the identity of Ho Chi Minh City. For example, one of their impulses is
"passion," or the role consumption and libidinal energies play in the
formation of identities (Amin and Thrift 2007: 147). However, despite
economists' insistence on the economic rationality of their argument, the
selfish, pleasure-seeking individual lies at the intersection of supply and
demand (Amin and Thrift 2007: 148), and it is here where this manu-

script's focus on entrepreneurialism intersects with the cultural-economy. Vietnam consists of the complicated interplay between political policies like đổi mới, actors pursuing their cultural-economic interests and the rules, rhythms, and established ways of doing business which frame cultural-economies. Modeling "objective" economic behaviors reduces these complexities into a replicable, uniform pattern of urban development and does not adequately address the Ho Chi Minh City economy in transition.

This book's view of value encompasses more than the materiality of economic transactions. That is, actor relations can find noneconomic yet meaningful value in objects and signs and alter them into objects and signs with enhanced noneconomic value. Actor-relations can also transform them into things with economic value. Items such as familial keepsakes or pictures (chapter 6), and places where pain and death are recalled (chapter 5) function beyond the level of economic value to tourism actors. Likewise the đổi mới policies, authored by the state, are objects without clear divisions between economic progress and cultural preservation/protection.

Moreover, this study also emphasizes culture at an expedient level, useful in attracting tourist consumers and the government's cultural offerings, which is an important distinction from the cultural practices identified in conducting business in Ho Chi Minh City. Culture is resourceful for tourism firms who understand that the presentation of national culture, cultural authenticity, and cultural practices contributes to their entrepreneurial niche, their collective bottom lines, increases the demand for their product lines, and enhances their capacity to promote themselves in the marketplace. But for Yúdice (2003) this is just the beginning of culture's power because while these firms understand capital's power and target it for exploitation they at the same time use it as "a foundation for resistance against that very same economic system" (2003: 6). As the national economic system continues to be dominated by SOEs, firms use forms of culture in innovative ways to oppose the proprietary regulations of the Vietnamese economy, regulations that themselves are often instituted by the state under the banner of Vietnamese national culture.

Thus, culture has a broad role in the Ho Chi Minh City tourism industry. It is a part of the local market, as when private companies appeal to local SOEs against rent-seeking. Recently, many of the city's private tourism firms banded together to plead to the Ho Chi Minh City government for a transparent, nonpartisan, third-party association where public and private tourism companies could share knowledge, strategize, and market the city against what has increasingly become a cutthroat urban tourism market in Southeast Asia. These private tourism companies used local relationships and channels to reach the local tourism authorities in their appeals to make competition between private and state-owned companies more equitable and fair through an association that serves every firm's needs. At an expedient level, culture is resourceful when drawing in tourists and their money. Some firms market their companies as eco-tourism companies, some promise a "quintessential" Vietnamese experience (including cooking demonstrations, home stays, and "back of the motorbike" tours), and others present Vietnam as a country that is perpetually "war torn" and attractive for its war sites. Culture is also useful at a level of identity, as in descriptions of what it means to be "Vietnamese" and "foreign" (chapter 6). However, this book minimizes looking at cultural resourcefulness as a finished product and instead traces how actors in the Ho Chi Minh City tourism sector arrive at understanding that certain forms of culture are resourceful, and how they are used in their dealings with other firms and in their presentation of options for tourists. Additionally, this study looks at the creative processes of actors and firms in their attachment of culture to objects and sites. Here culture is constructed rather than accessed.

Yet to have the state tell it, Vietnamese culture is homogenous and stable, a metaphysical system of beliefs and values hovering like a celestial body over the Vietnamese population and represented in the actions of its people. Vietnamese culture is a culture without a concrete foundation (see Duncan 1980). It does not seem to matter to the state that one cannot effectively point out any material things that compose national culture. The Vietnamese government prefers instead to keep national culture intentionally vague because it is more effective for the purposes of maintaining political control to identify what Vietnamese culture is not, or what is unacceptable in their country, rather than specify ontological things that compose national culture (Marr and Rosen 1999: 201). The relationship between the state's hollowed-out description of national culture and its deployment by Ho Chi Minh City private actors makes for a striking contrast with which to build this study. As is argued in chapter 3, the state's efforts to project a benign, impenetrable national culture have in reality been fraught with contradiction. In the đổi mới era, the state struggles with this paradox: how to frame national culture on the basis of "Vietnameseness" and "foreignness" when foreign economic investment is encouraged?

## PROJECT JUSTIFICATION AND STUDY POPULATION

*Outline of Study Population and Document Analysis*

This book draws largely from interviews with actors in the local tourism industry to understand the meanings and uses of entrepreneurship in Ho Chi Minh City. To begin with, tourism executives are unique actors because they can be seen as the primary producers and managers of the

Vietnamese "experience" in the tourism marketplace. In the hierarchical world of Vietnamese business, it is the tourism executive body who forges contacts with subsidiary businesses, plans tourism routes, negotiates rates with hoteliers, and educates tour guides and employees about the itineraries, policies, and business models their company's are to stand by.

As is shown in later chapters, tourism executives innovatively create Vietnamese history, develop tourism consumption activities, lean on long-standing notions of Vietnamese culture, and assess their own senses of culture to construct new entrepreneurial spaces of culture in the local tourism landscape. Tourism operators and employees, considered the second rung of tourism actor in the industry, are embodiments of the Vietnam that they represent: they can speak authoritatively of the country, they reflect the style of dress and mannerisms specific to the nation and its culture, and offer outsiders a window into Vietnamese "reality" through exclusive representations of place. Tourism operators and employees who do not interact with tourists on a daily basis nevertheless reproduce imaginaries in the construction of itineraries and destination points; email, phone, and fax exchanges; and in their arrangement of promotional materials heavily influenced by the relationship between specificities and local culture. These exhibitions are speculative in nature and are generated in order to compete for tourism revenue, but they also do something to establish certain methods of entrepreneurialism in the country. Tourism employees are thus more than purveyors of entrepreneurship; they are in a unique collective position to define and reproduce entrepreneurial activities, and to inject meanings of entrepreneurship and Vietnamese culture into objects, places, and people in the tourism landscape.

This study centers on private, or non-state employees in a number of private Ho Chi Minh City tour companies. By non-state I mean employees who do not work directly for the city. However, although Ho Chi Minh City tourism businesses are strictly defined by the state as either foreign operated, private, joint venture, state-run, or "illegal" (see Suntikul, Airey, and Butler 2008; Lloyd 2004), in reality the businesses transcend and usurp these categories in their business operations and networks. More will be said about the differences between these categories in the next chapter.

"Foreign-operated" tourism companies are far and away the least ambiguous of all of the categories of tourism player in the city. Between 2002 and 2014 I conducted interviews with employees from twenty foreign-operated companies, licensed by the Vietnamese government to have representative offices in Ho Chi Minh City. Additionally, I interviewed employees in eighteen private tourism companies (some of which have opened and closed during the period of my research). Private companies are defined as being owned and operated by Vietnamese proprietors unaffiliated with the state. Interestingly, none of these companies are legitimately "private" by Western business standards if by private we mean the freedom to ply the tourism trade under the established, transparent rules and regulations governing business generally and the tourism sector specifically. However, because the state coins these companies private, and because this characterization of a nonpublic company is understood in the Western world, I use private company to describe these businesses. Executives in private companies are routinely subjected to audits by the Ho Chi Minh City bureau of the Vietnamese National Administration of Tourism (VNAT), audits in which their contact lists, pricing models, tour routes, and accounting ledgers are taken, copied, and given to employees in state-owned companies. Employees of VNAT are also employees of state companies so the ruling tourism organization is both a regulator and a competitor in the Ho Chi Minh City tourism marketplace. On the other hand, private employees proactively seek out state-run companies and share or sell proprietary information to them in exchange for money, information on competitors, and other favors. Private executives "consult" on state-run tourism projects for fees and other bureaucratic advantages, such as the waiving of fees, preferential treatment for visa and permit applications, and so on. This is part of the "cultural" component of the Vietnamese cultural-economy that supports my research initiatives. While usually considered illegal activities in Western business practices, this give and take between public and private companies is the impetus for many Ho Chi Minh City business activities.

Given the difficulties procuring and growing a joint venture business, there are very few joint ventures involving tourism players in Ho Chi Minh City. Employees of three joint venture companies agreed to be interviewed for this study. During my period of research one of these companies transitioned to a foreign-operated company. Joint ventures are often subjected to extra fees, possible interference by various government agencies, and higher levels of supervision (by a multitude of firms and actors) that foreign-operated companies are usually not. Thus, the allure of transitioning to a foreign-operated company is always present in the city's tourism industry. On the other side of the coin, employees from long-standing and successful joint venture companies in Ho Chi Minh City tell me that the state partners are helpful in facilitating and fast-tracking permissions, offering advice and connecting players in the industry, and/or largely stay out of the joint venture's tourism model. There are therefore a range of relationships that seem to exist within the different joint venture tourism companies in Ho Chi Minh City today.

Despite frequent attempts, I was unable to interview any employees in SOE tourism companies during fieldwork in Ho Chi Minh City, save one interview with an employee at the city's division of VNAT. The reasons are many and multifaceted, but the major reason is the guarded nature of state rule and a trickle-down effect of caution to provincial and city governments, government organizations, and SOEs. Notwithstanding the breadth of deregulations occurring throughout every sector of the Vietnamese economy and as mentioned above, SOEs continue to enjoy preferential treatment by the Vietnamese state (Gainsborough 2010, 2003). SOEs benefit from inexpensive and no-bid land and construction deals, "fuzzy math" accounting, close contacts in all levels of government, a role in the regulatory structure of the sector they operate in, and decision-making capabilities, such as a say in which competitors can enter the market. This is so because the state, through its tourism SOEs, desires "to retain an active and substantive role in the economy (through control over the private sector, monopolisation of infrastructure and high-income-generating investments)" (Lloyd 2004: 198). In other words, the playing field does not necessarily favor private industry. While this is certainly changing, government agencies have largely chosen silence with me, and, it seems, with other social scientists conducting research in Vietnam as well (see Scott, Miller, and Lloyd 2006).

Due to these challenges, this manuscript uncovers the logic of the Vietnamese state through the language of the state's cultural đổi mới policies. I was directed to the National Archives and to a government website by the employee I interviewed at VNAT to read and translate the state's cultural policies during the reform era, and this material is covered in chapter 3. This documentation is not written especially for the Vietnamese tourism industry. Rather, it is a set of broad guidelines, reminders, decrees, and suggestions, which follows the ambiguity of the state's construction of culture I outlined earlier. The documentation is translated because it provides a state voice regarding national cultural policy. These papers reveal how the state understands proper entrepreneurship to be a community project aimed at promoting the goals of the Vietnamese people, with support and direction from the state. It outlines some general guidelines about what constitutes appropriate entrepreneurial activities and what are disruptive to the national fabric. It shares with its readers (albeit ambiguously) how Vietnamese culture serves as a central pillar of the country. Although local explanations of culture foreground my study, the đổi mới policies translated in this book do not simply serve as a static platform on which to consider local Ho Chi Minh City actor interpretations and presentations of culture. Rather, they counterpose local cultural and entrepreneurial appropriations and more fully illuminate the entrepreneurial character of the state.

Methods and Nature of Interviews

I gained access to tourism employees and their businesses through the "snowball" method, relying on existing contacts in the tourism industry to vouch for me and my project and facilitate introductions with others. I conducted sixty-five distinctive interviews while in Vietnam between

2002 and 2014 to support the research in this monograph. There were forty-two respondents, thirty of whom were men and twelve who were women. Interviews were both semistructured and structured based upon the request of the respondent. For semistructured interviews I tended to build off of a few ideas during each interview session. For example, one interview session may touch on the job responsibilities of the respondent; some may center on the entrepreneurial leeway executives and employees have in setting business agendas; another session may concern personal definitions of Vietnamese culture; and sometimes interviews centered on family health, lineage, and my interest in Vietnam.

Structured and semistructured interviews were both conducted in the language the respondent felt most comfortable in (usually English, sometimes in Vietnamese, and often in a mix of both languages). While in offices, notes were taken during interviews and audiorecording was largely shunned. Similarly, on the occasions when I was invited to respondent homes or to meet outside of work, I recorded only rarely; Ho Chi Minh City is generally a very loud city and background noise often affects audiorecordings. In these cases I wrote extensive notes and cross-checked their accuracy with respondents after they were transcribed.

There is a disparity in interviewees across gender lines. In the first place, a majority of the city's tour guides are male. Given this study's interest in the presentational and performative aspects of the tourism industry, a lot of my interviewees are (male) guides. Female tourism employee contacts were accessed largely through word-of-mouth conversations (rather than meeting on tours, for example). I also participated in formal and informal company meetings, traveled with employees on fact-finding missions throughout south Vietnam, and took twenty day-trip tours from Ho Chi Minh City to various spots in south Vietnam. The bulk of this fieldwork was conducted over 2006, when I held a Fulbright Graduate Research Fellowship in Vietnam.

## OUTLINE OF CHAPTERS

In chapter 2, I develop a cultural-economic entrepreneurial framework for understanding the Vietnamese economy during the reform era using examples from the Ho Chi Minh City tourism sector. I incorporate scholarship from geography, cultural studies, and international business to further my argument that an underdeveloped yet integral component of Asian business includes an entrepreneurial spirit among individual business people and the firms they represent.

In chapter 3, I review the Vietnam government's relationship with national culture in a paradigmatic epoch in Vietnam's history, the đổi mới era. The foundations of resistance, equitability, and revolutionary thought in the state's policies correlate with the discourses developed by

SOEs in the Ho Chi Minh City tourism industry. They assert the state's need to retain political and economic control over Vietnam. Further, I review the contradictions inherent in national culture and state efforts to untangle these problems into a coherent set of dictums. This chapter's general argument rests on the notion that the state uses Vietnamese culture to invoke national difference or uniqueness, which legitimates its leadership. I reject claims that postsocialist states are forced down an inevitable path toward neoliberalization and offer an alternative understanding of postsocialist governance in which the Vietnamese government expects the global economy to conform to its own unique brand of market socialism.

Chapter 4 draws from interview data to link entrepreneurialism to tourism in Ho Chi Minh City. Using evidence from employees and firms in Ho Chi Minh City, I show how entrepreneurial relationships are built less on the distinctions between state and non-state enterprise and more on a combination of market opportunities and existing or burgeoning cultural relations that also incorporate tourist consumers.

Chapter 5 evaluates commonplace war tourism sites and boutique offerings to sites associated with what is likely Vietnam's most important tourism niche—the "Vietnam" War outside of Vietnam and the "American" War inside it—to show how these landscapes dissolve the binary between tourist producer-tourism consumer. In these case studies, seemingly typical, stable roles for tourism producers and tourists like insider/outsider, knowledgeable/gullible, and poor/wealthy have little explanatory merit because tourist producers and tourists bring different knowledges to play in the war landscape, knowledges that do not align with conventional understandings of tourism producer-tourist consumer relations. What makes this argument important is that the war, instead of being understood as a living tourist memorial to differences between the East and West, is used as a binding agent for tourist producers and tourists alike. The state's involvement in the production of war sites in Vietnam is also considered. For government officials, war sites are used to extend the argument that Vietnamese culture is used in times of invasion, cohering Vietnamese people against external threat.

Chapter 6 investigates the ranks of Vietnamese and Asian tourists visiting Vietnam with the goal of upsetting traditional notions of "representative" Western tourist activities associated with sight-seeing, relaxation, and comfort. Asian tourists visiting Vietnam make up the lion's share of overseas tourists visiting Vietnam today yet they do not conform to predictable tourist behaviors long understood to be driven from the outside and do not intend to participate in the general activities set into place by state-run agencies and, to a lesser extent, private or non-state tourism firms. This encourages tourist producer entrepreneurs to create unique offerings and abandon less conventional offerings, adding a new twist to the idea of entrepreneurial endeavors in tourism in Vietnam.

With the twin phenomena of the recent global economic crisis (which has battered Western, overseas tourist visits to Vietnam) and the growing numbers of middle-class Asian tourists, Vietnam's government and entrepreneur base has been forced to ditch established tourism excursions and establish new options for Asian tourists, thereby transforming the Vietnamese tourism marketplace by enrolling new forms of expertise and knowledge and abandoning irrelevant or unprofitable forms along the way. This chapter highlights the malleability of "typical" tourist behaviors as well as the versatility of the entrepreneurial experience among Vietnamese tourist producers in a century that likely will be marked by the rise of the Asian tourist (Minca and Oakes 2011, Singh 2009, Winter, Teo, and Chang 2009).

The concluding chapter broadens the discussion from the Vietnam experience to examine the impact of tourism and the leisure economy on transitional economies and nonrepresentative governments in Asia. Using evidence from Malaysia and Cambodia (among others), I show how tourism presents Asian countries' governments with a paradox: by putting the country "up for sale" and commodifying it for tourist consumption, national governments face more challenges in maintaining their control over their political authority. Therefore, Asian governments such as the ones above have shifted from command governance in which political and economic authority goes unquestioned to an entrepreneurial form of governance that is proactive in establishing new types of leisure opportunities that diversify their economic holdings and include messages that buttress their political authority.

# TWO

## Rethinking Entrepreneurialism through Cultural-Economic Registers

### INTRODUCTION

In this chapter I outline a hybrid cultural-economic approach to assess growth in the tourism industry in Ho Chi Minh City. Additionally, I stress the importance of investigating the Ho Chi Minh City tourism industry from the bottom-up rather than from a "top-down" urban state-centric perspective. In Vietnam, a "bottom-up" approach does not necessarily neglect state actors: the blurriness of the boundaries between the "public" and "private" in the everyday negotiation of profit and sales in the tourism industry is emphasized here.

As mentioned in the opening chapter, one effect of Vietnam's đổi mới policies is the decentralization of political power to local governments (Gainsborough 2010; 2003). Government leaders in Ho Chi Minh City now enjoy greater decision-making capacity than ever before, a trait that is featured in urban-led development strategies in countries around the world. This power shift would seem to pit Ho Chi Minh City officials' political objectives against the economic goals of Ho Chi Minh City's non-state, private tourism firms. For example, urban political leaders may deem certain tourism sites to be off limits to tourists if they represent sensitive aspects of Vietnam's past (such as war memorials, war cemeteries, or unofficial memorials honoring Vietnamese military who served in the Republic of Vietnam, South Vietnam's military forces during the American war). However, Ho Chi Minh City government officials and private tourism actors must also bring together their disparate goals for the purposes of selling the city to consumers. As an overseas Vietnamese-Australian owner of a boutique private tourism company named Diệp explained to me, "We have to understand the attitude of different cultures for our tourism business, but we also have to understand the local culture in the government. Our responsiveness to them is key (for our success)." Thus, coordination between public and private sectors is an important tenet of the entrepreneurial strategies underpinning the city's urban governance that deserves more attention than what existing work on entrepreneurial cities in the West and Asia has already provided. Players in the Ho Chi Minh City government and the city's private actors progress through an uneasy yet necessary relationship, driven by their need to harmonize their different goals to recruit and please tourist visitors but who are at the same time separated by dramatic differences and goals. This is nuance that is lacking in most studies of urban entrepreneurialism and little understood in tourism studies, especially in Asia (Winter, et al. 2009).

Lastly, the commodification of culture is a fundamental part of an entrepreneurial city (Su 2015, Raco and Gilliam 2012). For both the Ho Chi Minh City government and tourism producers, the sale of culture is a fundamental part of their daily operations. They sell activities like day trips to the Mekong Delta, visits to the Cu Chi Tunnels, and photo-taking at the Central Post Office, among other offerings. In light of these findings, and despite not being a Western city, Ho Chi Minh City can be considered an entrepreneurial city, though not without the need to adjust to it to be less "economic" and more "cultural" in character.

The cultural-economy approach to cities favors values, norms, impulses and experiences of urban livelihoods (as well as the economic transactions themselves) that entangle the cultural with the economic. Said another way, classic understandings of urban entrepreneurialism tends to derive power from a generalizable, replicable set of relationships between urban governments and private capital where private capital is dominant. In the case of the cultural-economic approach to cities, urban orders illustrate a hybrid cultural-economy and drive the intertwinement of the terms. These orders, frequently explained under the banner of a rational market, are driven by irrationality, impulse, serendipity, and comfort, along with the more evident yet ever-changing standards of urban market economies associated with production, consumption, and the distribution of goods. Economic transactions, so often understood as two rational actors engaging in a mutually beneficial action based on the laws of supply and demand, are in actuality imbued and maintained by habits of reciprocity and rules governed by forms of sociability (Amin and Thrift 2007: 143) that are not reducible to economic transactions. In Ho Chi Minh City, informal relationships between tourism actors condition their economic transactions. Financial cost benefits take a backseat to trustworthiness and being able to vouch for the integrity (financial and otherwise) of a potential partner. One midlevel employee at a private tourism company told me that one of the ways he trains his staff is to take a group of tour guides out to dinner with members of his family. On these occasions he "tests" them by observing how they interact together. This exercise, Duy explained to me, impresses upon his guides that the respectful, friendly, and patient manner they express toward his family must be similar to how they engage with tourists. According to Duy, he wants his guests to feel "like part of a Vietnamese family." For Duy and others in the tourism industry, divorcing issues of trust, values, and power (to name a few) from the economy hampers our understandings of the complexities of the everyday urban cultural-economy as well as for imagining new ways in which the urban economy may be captured.

Imagining a new way in which the urban economy is practiced and experienced means that a universally applicable methodology favoring the economic is unsatisfactory. I argue that an urban economy cannot be delimited into specific "stages" of capitalism, as much of the literature on urban entrepreneurship argues, because stages (e.g., precapitalist, emergent, advanced capitalist) have no clear cut boundaries in a city like Ho Chi Minh City, which has arguably had as long a "free market" backbone—through colonialism to the transitional period between French and American occupation to today's booming metropolis (Peycam 2013 and see Sasges and Cheshier 2012)—as other Western capitalist cities. Tracing the lines where advanced capitalism begins and intermediate or burgeoning capitalism ends are problematic at best and useless at worst because economic practices are shot through with an assortment of cultural inputs at a variety of points in a market-based contract. Even in cities such as Ho Chi Minh City whose leaders claim a "socialist" free-market system, the rich array of economic transactions that feed the city's economy are built on an equally rich tangle of values, power relations, economic knowledges, and negotiated conditions of reciprocity. Economic benefits are just one aspect of these relationships. Thus, it is less helpful to assume certain cities fit into the category of "capitalism" or "socialism" than it is to ask how market transactions take on different temperaments given the cultural-economic impulses that support them. In what follows, I bring seven registers highlighted by Amin and Thrift (2007, 2004) to bear on the Ho Chi Minh City tourism sector in order to illustrate how the city's entanglements between the cultural and the economic unfold.

## HO CHI MINH CITY'S URBAN ENTREPRENEURIALISM UNDER THE LENS OF CULTURAL-ECONOMY

The first register moves beyond the real/representation binary and instead depicts the passions of those involved in the drive to sustain capitalism (2007: 147). In entrepreneurial cities, urban entrepreneurs are passionate in their quest to fill cities with creative designations and their pockets with cash. In the case of Ho Chi Minh City, I interviewed a private tourism operator named Đức who was lamenting the lack of cultural offerings in the city as compared to Hanoi, Vietnam's capital. He recounted his meetings with the city's government officials and his attempts to strategize alongside the government to develop the city's tourism sector:

> (Ho Chi Minh City) city government leaders are not in line with the tourism industry's potential here. Ho Chi Minh City is usually the last spot on tourist trips, leaving one or two days of shopping only. Ninety percent of (foreign) tourists begin their trip in Hanoi, not here, and work their way down the country, ending it here. All of their money is spent and there is nothing to see in Saigon. It's boring here. Saigon's government leaders aren't in line with the cultural interests people have. Hanoi has water puppet theatres, historical buildings, museums, beautiful vistas and lakes. You can tour Hanoi for a week and not visit all of their cultural sites. Also, Hanoi sells the same tourism goods and trinkets that our city does. What do we have? Asking the city government to build new cultural sites is like asking for free money. They say that Ho Chi Minh (City) is a business hub, not a tourist hub like Hanoi!

Other research has shown that the Ho Chi Minh City government is entrepreneurial as it selectively chooses which businesses and entrepreneurs it chooses to do business with (as the numerous jointly held hotels and tourism businesses attest, see Gainsborough 2010). Đức is undoubtedly frustrated with the lack of tourism offerings in the city. He wants the city to have more imageries of the city that fulfill tourist desires to take home representations of the "real" city. He is also upset that the monthly meetings he has with the city government have not sparked city government leaders to feel the "libidinal energies that motivate entrepreneurs, speculators and investors" (Amin and Thrift 2007: 147) to facilitate new tourist sites, sounds, and moods to attract tourists and their consumptive needs. In my interviewee's mind the city has been constructed by city planners as a global business center, not a tourism center. The process by which an entrepreneurial economy is produced must have the "compulsion of consumption" (*ibid.*) by foreign tourists but it also must have the allegiant desires of the Ho Chi Minh City public-private coordinative relationship to direct physical and symbolic city transformations of the city. For Đức passion is imperative to the "producer-consumer relations on which capitalist success is delicately balanced" (Amin and Thrift 2007: 147–148). He experiences the desirous motivations to consume everyday when he takes tourists through Ho Chi Minh City and Vietnam, but he finds his passion to produce a more attractive urban consumptive landscape wanting in his relations with the city government. Accounting for the passions, unrequited or otherwise, in a public-private urban relationship allows for a more completed version of urban entrepreneurialism because it captures the similar energies of urban producers in fulfilling their multifaceted desires.

A second register is moral values. Moral values identify business practices with certain understood (yet unstable) ethical expectations, imbuing exchange with more than just the dry mechanisms of supply and demand in a market economy. Economic life becomes coded with nonmonetary valuations of judgment and deservingness (*ibid*. 148). Moral values "include work emphasizing the orders of moral justification that naturalize particular forms of economic conduct (e.g., hedonism or individualism versus restraint or collective responsibility, fast versus slow food, trade versus aid, project-oriented versus task-oriented worth)" (*ibid*.). Since the advent of đổi mới Ho Chi Minh City's planners have juggled their worth to the state as, on the one hand, a leading economic producer and on the other its costs as a site of cultural hedonism and selfish individuality. In an edited book on culture and urban Vietnam since the reform period, two Vietnamese scholars weighed in on the cultural degradation of Ho Chi Minh City's morality after the introduction of đổi mới: "The policy of đổi mới has transformed the city, reviving its long forgotten image as the 'Pearl of the Orient.' However, market reforms have also contributed to a growing polarization between rich and poor, resulting in the degradation of moral values and the deterioration of personal as well as social relationships" (Dang and Pham 2003: 197). Ho Chi Minh City's entrepreneurs take on vast amounts of risk when undertaking entrepreneurial projects with judgments of this kind coloring Vietnamese investor sentiments outside of the city. Similarly, some who are "inside" Ho Chi Minh City feel that the city's morality has taken a precipitous plunge after Vietnam's transformation to "market socialism." On the other hand, the state made a noteworthy decision in 2006 to elect a successful Ho Chi Minh City businessman named Nguyễn Minh Triết as the president of the country, the first head of state from south Vietnam since Vietnam's reunification in 1975. Triết's business empire—built out of the đổi mới policies' free market ideals—signaled to many Vietnamese the acceptance of the "southern" way of doing business in the country. The contradictions between Ho Chi Minh City's moral degradation and its value as an economic powerhouse beg further study in an entrepreneurial context.

A story circulating around the city's tourism industry recently relayed to me narrates the importance of moral values in the city's tourism activities. A recent and rapid increase in Malaysian and Indonesian tourists in Ho Chi Minh City has meant a subtle but not insignificant transformation of the city's downtown tourism environment. For example, halal restaurants dot the neighborhoods surrounding Ben Thanh market, there are a number of midrange and high-end hotels that now advertise exclusively to these communities, and there are a range of handicraft shops specializing in items that are advertised as being designed and produced by Vietnam's Cham Muslim population. In one instance indicating the attuned and contextual nature of moral values as they pertain to tourist guests, a

Malaysian Muslim dignitary hosted a halal dinner banquet catered by a restaurant owned by a Vietnamese tour operator. The food was to be prepared in accordance with Muslim dietary preferences. After the Vietnamese tour company leader welcomed the dignitary and his guests, he or she subsequently walked into the kitchen to make sure all of the food preparations were in order for the evening. To his or her horror, the kitchen staff was mixing order preparations from the main dining room (including pork) with orders from the private dining room. The tour director insisted that the kitchen staff discard over two thousand U.S. dollars worth of food while he frantically tried to salvage an edible dinner for his Malaysian guests.

I heard this story a number of times in recent months in early 2015 by a number of different tour operators in the city, and in each case the story was told in an anxious, almost fearful manner. The implication behind this story is that morality in the entrepreneurial marketplace means more than making sure the "market rate" for a given product or service is agreed upon and monetary debts are paid in a timely fashion: moral values include being culturally sensitive, aware, and responsive to a variety of different habits, norms, and values from a wealth of different types of tourist.

A third register is economic knowledge. Economic knowledge on its own cannot be identified solely with a cultural-economic approach because their version of economic knowledge concerns aspects of innovation and learning (see McFarlane 2011). What distinguishes the economic knowledge register in cultural-economy is the actor-networks that drive forms of capitalism (Amin and Thrift 2007: 148). These are drives that are built by the amalgamation of human and nonhuman actors to align and assemble themselves. Amin and Thrift embrace the fluidities of networks and their abilities to foster societal change in urban life (Amin and Thrift 2007: 148).

For example, even when the relationship is based on the privileging of the state in the local tourism community, public and private coordination continues apace. The city tourism bureau mentioned earlier serves as a representation of the fractious but necessary coordinative relationships between the public and private tourism sectors. It is important here to note that the pooling of resources, ideas, and strategies for the economic betterment of the city do not always foster increased allegiances and trustworthiness, and that entrepreneurial relationships have vastly different goals and temperaments. Public-private coordination constructs more than "patterns of sociality and identity formation in communities of joint practice of various kinds" (Amin and Thrift 2007: 148), including blockages, but economic knowledge is a beneficial conceptual alternative to an impermeable, economically determinant model in the study of urban entrepreneurialism.

In Ho Chi Minh City, economic knowledge is valuable for guides when they negotiate economic relationships with tourists and tour companies of different backgrounds and markets. For example, a tour guide named Trâm shared with me that she is more comfortable working with Western tourists than Asian tourists because "Western tourists tip more money" than their Asian counterparts. Notwithstanding the different findings arising from Hoang's study of Western and Asian businessmen in Ho Chi Minh City (Hoang 2015), Trâm's is the kind of economic knowledge that is not gained in the classroom or in the process of becoming certified as a tour guide. She learns about these tendencies through regular tour guide work, conversations with members of the tourism community, and an awareness of the most valuable currencies circulating through the Ho Chi Minh City economy (U.S. dollars, for example, are preferred over other currencies).

Another tour guide named Binh told me that, contra Trâm, she prefers to be contracted to work for tour companies that cater to east Asian tourist guests—and in particular South Korean and Japanese tourists—because they are respectful, inquisitive, and quiet. She added that they are very prepared tourists in that they are knowledgeable about the various cultural sites and top restaurants in the city. What is important in this narrative is not whether Binh's understanding of nation-dependent forms of economic knowledge are accurate or not but how she prescribes particular notions of place knowledge superiority on certain types of tourist and adjusts her employment choices on this basis.

Another register is trust. Intimacy and mutual interdependence form the social milieu for many economic goals in urban Vietnam, highlighted by the research of numerous Vietnamese studies scholars (Hoang 2015, Schwenkel 2014, Voelkner 2014, Schwenkel and Leshkowich 2012, Truitt 2012). It often seems that trust reigns supreme in business dealings throughout Ho Chi Minh City, where historical connections, kinship ties, and friendship determine economic coordination rather than letting potential monetary profitability shape future interpersonal relationships. Amin and Thrift argue that trust "both sustains economic transactions as well as mobilizes creative energies based on mutuality and reciprocity" (2007: 148). These twin impetuses are place-specific to Ho Chi Minh City, where the perception is that the possibilities of the market economy take precedence over the dynamics of trust and trustworthiness, convoluting a Vietnam-centric approach to the economy that in many ways is built on interpersonal, informal relations. In my research, entrepreneurs are keen to develop closer ties with foreign investors based on the potential of the city's tourism market but are hamstrung by official controls on foreign direct investment based on cultural skepticisms that foreign companies and their employees have neocolonial intentions. As it stands now (in 2015), Ho Chi Minh City tourism entrepreneurs use kinship ties with their relatives and other Vietnamese overseas people in the United States,

Australia, and Europe to introduce them to international business contacts, contacts that are themselves supported by long-standing ties and mutual histories (Nguyen 2012, Small 2012).

In an everyday sense, the Ho Chi Minh City tourism industry revolves around the intersection of trust and safety. Much like tourist needs around the world, tourists in Ho Chi Minh City arguably place the most value on traveling safely from one place to the next, consuming food that will not make them ill, and being cognizant of potential issues involving street conflict when they are by themselves. Thus, the tour company's role is first and foremost to keep tourists safe and in Ho Chi Minh City this involves introducing tourists to the hazards of the city's often lawless and chaotic motorbike transport culture; showing them what and where to go to find the right combination of delicious, "clean," authentic, and local cuisine; and steering them away from potential danger. In return to keeping tourists "safe" in a myriad of ways tour companies are rewarded with a strong safety record and business has the potential to bloom. Companies that seriously and continuously violate tourists' sense of trust must face not only declining revenue and reputation but censure from the Ho Chi Minh City Department of Culture, Sports, and Tourism. Censure can include fines, suspension of tour licensing, and in extreme cases, closure. Trust therefore holds a multifaceted role in the production of the Ho Chi Minh City tourism industry. Moreover, the urban cultural-economy lends itself to thinking about the various ways trust links, unsettles, and transcends relationships between public and private tourism actors.

Fifth in this list of registers or impulses is the role of evolution in the cultural-economy (Amin and Thrift 2007: 149). Amin and Thrift cite Castree's study of the categories of culture and economy (Castree 2004) in driving the emergence of what comes to be known as the cultural-economy. For my purposes, innovative techniques among actors in the Ho Chi Minh City economy have an appearance that closely mirrors the kinds of entrepreneurial creations evident in Western cities such as the marketing and promotion of the city "as a favorable environment for business and leisure as 'market-place' politics become predominant" (Hall and Hubbard 1998: 6). There are many reasons why these similarities could be occurring. One possibility may be due to the historical influence of French and American interests in south Vietnam. It could also be due to the installation of Western-stylized educational systems under colonial rule that engender certain definitions of culture and economy that translate well to the sale of leisure to foreign consumers. An interrogation of aspects of a coevolution of the terms culture and economy in Ho Chi Minh City and Western cities would be a fruitful intellectual undertaking and would place Ho Chi Minh City's entrepreneurial goals in a historical, colonial context, expanding urban entrepreneurialism to include elements of subservience, learned behaviors, and methods of innovative resistance under its canon.

The sixth register outlines the organization of power in the control of the mechanisms of the economy. While Marxist analyses have proven that modes of power written into everyday practices of capitalism protect and perpetuate specific economic interests (Amin and Thrift 2007: 149), other scholars now argue that economies are often scripted to prioritize the "cognitive" and delegitimate the "expressive" (Allen 2002: 39). Urban entrepreneurial projects often have the appearance of being playful and emotive while the products are the outcome of a rationally minded urban intelligentsia. This paradox is often intentionally scripted by urban leaders to extend their own financial interests while categorizing the projects themselves as belonging "to the people." In Ho Chi Minh City urban entrepreneurs tag entrepreneurial ventures with the Vietnamese state's political mantra "rich people, strong nation, civilized and equitable society" (*dân giàu, nước mạnh, xã hội văn minh*), playing off of Vietnam's socialist ideals as they dot the city with new and highly profitable hotels, shopping centers, and office buildings.

The final register in Amin and Thrift's reading of the cultural-economy is the standardization of different economies into an emblematic reading of the economy throughout the world. Taken-for-granted assumptions about the primacy of the service economy in global economics, the heightened use of symbols to give meaning to the economy, and characteristics of entrepreneurialism in urban economies around the world have all become common drivers of the economy. Emblematic readings of the economy minimize variation (Amin and Thrift 2007: 149) and allow for self-fulfilling prophesies of economic transformation. In cities around the world entrepreneurialism is often seen as an inevitable condition of governance no matter what political structure individual cities take. As mentioned earlier, Ho Chi Minh City is cast as Vietnam's economic powerhouse that is built on the backs of the service and information economies. Ho Chi Minh City's coordinative enterprises are thus presumed to be just like any other city's in the world. These presumptions lead to certain disconnects and failures when investors attempt to do business with Ho Chi Minh City companies and find that "their version" of entrepreneurialism is not "in line" with global standards (see Hoang 2015). A few non-Vietnamese private tourism employees I interviewed from Vietnam remarked on the difficulties in coordinating with the city government on coordinative projects, while Vietnamese private tourism company employee responses were mixed on the subject. Mythical "ideal types" of commerce and business deals form the basis for economic understandings of the urban marketplace but do not always fit the mold in localized economic practice.

Anh, a longtime manager of the Ho Chi Minh City branch of a foreign-owned tourism company, explained to me very bluntly that their company's strategy is very simple: "When the government tells my company what to do, we do it." When I asked her if her company ever "experiments" with (for example) new tourist offerings, she told me that in the tourism sector "everyone knows each other. Generally, every company offers the same product (as other companies). Our company is a little bit different because we give the guest a better experience, but we are like all companies in Ho Chi Minh City: we take guests to the museum (War Remnant's Museum), the (Cu Chi) tunnels, the (Reunification) palace, the post office. It is true that there isn't variety for the tourist, but that is changing." From Anh's comments we are left to believe that there is an replication throughout the tourist economy in Ho Chi Minh City as companies compete on the quality of the guest experience rather than on innovative offerings and itineraries. This point would seem to challenge the inevitability of entrepreneurialism in the city. However, for as much as there is a sense of standardization of product offerings, there is also a strong motivation to behave in an entrepreneurial fashion. These two seemingly incongruous facets—standardization of product offerings and an entrepreneurial spirit among players in the tourism industry—sit side by side in the urban cultural-economy of Ho Chi Minh City.

Moreover, when taken together, passions, moral values, economic knowledge, trust, evolution, power, and economic standardization force a rethinking of urban entrepreneurialism based on the entanglement of culture and economy such that one of these aspects cannot be divorced from or rendered determinant to the other.

## CONCLUSION

Cultural-economy separates two conditions of social life that must now be seen as a complex entanglement of processes, meanings, imaginations, discourses, and practices. Cultural-economy is such a complex term that it helps to disassociate strict definitions of cultural-economy from some of its referents. Culture does not serve as a particular means of reasoning out the economy, nor is culture only a particular sector (among many) of the economy. Cultural-economy should not only point to the production of cultural or creative industries, such as the arts, because there seem to be no limits to naming something material or symbolic cultural by industries as diverse as furniture makers, airline food suppliers, and universities. The economy is not a particular kind of culture devoted specifically to fiscal transactions. Nor is the cultural-economy simply an ontological level of identification that allows us to explain certain practices, industries, and relationships as cultural or economic (or both) in nature. One cannot benefit from investigating the term "cultural-economy" to reinforce culture's various meanings because it would leave the complexities of the economy in the lurch. Lastly, we can run ourselves ragged railing against a singular (capitalist) economy in sole control of our lives (Gibson-Graham 2006) and thereby sufficiently neglect culture's constitutions in those very claims. For these reasons, beginning studies of cities and their processes with the recognition of the inextricability of culture and economy in all its forms, levels, and representations permits a number of heretofore neglected lines of inquiry and provides a kind of conceptual precision in line with the actualities of everyday economic life that are largely unimaginable under an economically determinant model of urban governance.

The everyday processes by which culture and economy are entangled in cities calls into question an advanced capitalist prerequisite for cities that engage in entrepreneurial governance. A hybridized cultural-economy encourages urban researchers to begin our analysis by asking, "How do we rethink different spheres of the urban economy (like consumption and production) and aspects of urban economic purpose and outcome (like competitiveness and innovation) in light of the entanglement of the culture and economy?" (Amin and Thrift 2007: 150), while purely economically minded scholars would likely prefer to ask, "To what degree are cities advanced in their capitalisms? How do these capitalisms reflect the entrepreneurial city model's tenets?" Most importantly, modeling an "appropriate" entrepreneurial city type reinforces the power of capital over cities and is therefore limited in scope and impact. The cultural-economy approach asks scholars to drop their commonplace assumptions of the economy and embrace the intertwinement of culture and economy in the daily survival and well-being of urban residents. "Modeling" an ideal entrepreneurial city resembles scientific modeling, with a hypothesis, testing, and a structured methodology. The cultural-economy approach dips into the rhythms and impulses of individuals and communities in their construction of the cultural-economy. If a cultural-economic approach to Ho Chi Minh City is taken we can analyze it on its own terms and with its own important architecture, pulses, and gatherings. With the global economy seemingly ruling everything from personal livelihoods to national governments to global processes such as cultural homogenization and neoliberalism, it is important to find an approach that questions economic inputs as economic, and one that builds a theory from the complexities of social life and not, like many studies today, from abstraction and consistency.

# THREE

## A Battle Worth Winning?

*The Production and Protection of Culture in the Reform Era*

### INTRODUCTION

As the sole representative of the Vietnamese government, the Communist Party of Vietnam is in a position to create, administer, and pronounce "national culture" to the Vietnamese population. Their variety of national culture is a uniquely Vietnamese system, fixed in time and resistant to outside influence, seen concurrently as a powerful, supervisory force on Vietnamese ideologies and on citizens' daily livelihoods. This chapter begins the empirical portion of the book by examining the ambiguous, contradictory, and yet very powerful cultural side of the state's đổi mới policies. It starts from the "top" (or from the state's cultural schemes) before using the later chapters to investigate more fully the "ground-up" conceptualizations of the cultural-economy in the tourism industry among entrepreneurs today. While there is no doubt that the economic aspects of the đổi mới policies have been central to Vietnam's state-building project after the end of the subsidy period in 1986, the cultural policies similarly are written with state political and economic expediency in mind. And yet the reform era's cultural policies have not enjoyed the levels of critical attention that the economic policies have (butsee Nguyễn-võ [2008] for a discussion of the reform period and social evils). It is the aim of this chapter to address this gap in research and to contextualize the state's version(s) of culture against private actor uses of the concept considered later in the manuscript. More specifically, my intention is to show that culture is not only a driver of locally based entrepreneurial tactics but part and parcel of the political framework of the Vietnamese state. Relatedly, the historical milieu of "official" uses of culture is also entertained in this chapter.

Indeed, a look into the đổi mới cultural policy package of today presents a picture that corresponds closely to the cultural movements of a newly formed Vietnamese government and led by the party in 1945. At both junctures in the country's history an expedient national culture has been invoked as a means to assert the state's power over the populace. The chapter assesses the early cultural proclamations that the new government staged in 1945 against those invoked today to counter the possibility of losing political power. In showing the similarities between the state's relationship to national culture through the early independence period and during the market reform era this chapter shares sympathies with Sasges and Cheshier's research revealing the continuity among the political economies of the French colonial regime and the current Vietnamese government (2012).

September 2, 1945, signaled the creation of a unified Democratic Republic of Vietnam that was unhinged from colonial rule and ostensibly free to operate as a sovereign nation. September 2 remains Vietnam's independence (quốc khánh) day and is annually venerated with much pageantry throughout the country. Though the date continues to be memorialized, the writings of Vietnamese historians produced during 1945 reflect the struggle, and ultimate failure, to establish a cohesive national cultural identity. The đổi mới policies are likewise an "independence" of sorts, representing a clear economic swing outward after more than a decade of political and economic isolationism. No less severe a shift for Vietnam, this contemporary era of đổi mới has created new anxieties for some members of the state who feel that Vietnam's cultural character has eroded during political and economic reform. A quote by Marr and Rosen confirms cadre misgivings from the current era: "Elderly revolutionaries routinely express worries about today's youth losing interest in the nation's proud history, to the extent that Vietnam's existence may be threatened once again by a national inferiority complex and a tendency to 'rent ourselves out to others,' rather than self-strengthening. Concerns like this have prompted the Vietnamese state in recent years to become more concerned than a couple of decades ago in claiming to defend and preserve authentic Vietnamese tradition and 'national culture'" (1999: 181). The contradictions that have arisen between economic development and national cultural maintenance are not easily rectifiable primarily because the state has heavily promoted the country's economic improvements since the introduction of đổi mới, and the state has identified itself as the creator of the policies (Beeson and Hung 2012). If đổi mới is an instrument designed to revive the national economy, how is national culture used to make sure economic development does not get in the way of the state's political command?

The chapter commences with a discussion of some expressions of Vietnamese national culture. The ambiguities and contradictions of Vietnamese culture have been intentionally constructed by the state as their leaders see potential damage or threats to their political and economic rule. The chapter then turns to an examination of culture's resourcefulness to the new government in the days following Japan's surrender to the Allied Forces in August, 1945, a month in which Japan's departure from Vietnam facilitated a national Communist rise to power. Here "culture-as-resource" does not mean national culture is necessarily coherent or retains any internal logic. Culture is resourceful precisely because it is malleable in design and execution (Yúdice 2003). Culture-as-resource is a specific type of culture that is artificially created and ambiguous, but it is one that the state claims sole purchase on in order to assert and expand its power. In other words, culture must take the form of resource in order to be useful to the state, and 1945 is the first indication of the efforts put forth by Vietnam's political leaders to use culture to assert its political authority.

The wording in the cultural policy document of the present extends beyond the creation of a new government in 1945 and focuses on the state's cultural battles of today. These battles, unlike the colonial battles the Vietnamese state was recovering from in 1945, are waged on production lines, in manufacturing plants, and in storefronts throughout the country. In no uncertain terms official language from ruling leadership in Hanoi posits a Vietnamese culture predetermined to shape the country's current and future socioeconomic development plans. The author of the document under scrutiny (Lê Khả Phiêu, the former General Secretary of the Communist Party of Vietnam from 1997 to 2001) has based culture on another in a long line of national "revolutions." As a primary representative of the state, Phiêu draws on the government's longheld if ambivalent militarized concepts such as community, patriotism, and independence to further inoculate the populace with a fighting spirit. The cultural policy document sheds light on the potential for the state's loss of political control as a member of the global economy in much the same way cadre members felt trepidation as they maneuvered through their reign over the country in and beyond 1945. In the conclusion I forecast that Vietnamese culture will continue to be strictly processed by the state in order to maintain single-party political leadership in the country.

## DEFINING CULTURE IN VIETNAM: A VIEW FROM "ABOVE"

Culture's meanings to the state are myriad and long-standing, and culture's importance to the government's view of national will is indisputable. But just what is Vietnamese national culture? For the purposes of this chapter it is important to discover Vietnamese culture through the

state's many usages of the term. There are numerous places designated
and promoted as cultural. "Văn hoá" (culture) is emblazoned on signs
throughout the country: "(family name) văn hóa" in front of family
homes, meaning "here resides a cultural family"; "ấp văn hoá," signifies
a cultural settlement or holding and is visible on signs in front of large
agricultural plots; "xã văn hóa" means cultural village and is displayed
as one arrives in a small town or community; "làng văn hóa" means
cultural village (again) and is also displayed at the entrance to a small,
rural community; "hẻm văn hóa," which means cultural alley, is visible
on many street corners in Vietnamese cities; "khu phố văn hóa" means
cultural quarter or square and is used on signs in urban neighborhoods,
and so on. Cultural status is designated to families by the local official
cadre if, for example, parents do not fight with each other for a period of
X months, husbands do not beat their wives, no member of the family is a
drug addict or a prostitute, the family is well-respected in the community, and sometimes (though not always) the family must be members of
the ruling class. Similar rules govern the appropriation of cultural vil-
lages, cultural alleys, and so on, all having to do with the congeniality
and honorable character of individuals and communities (no illegal gambling, no unregistered businesses, no criticism of the state, etc.). There do
not seem to be any tangible prizes to these awards beyond their symbolic
value.

Besides enhancing places, national uses of Vietnamese culture include
some common characteristics if measured by their recurrence in the national lexicon. One prominent one, and an idea that is repeated throughout this chapter's analysis is Vietnamese revolution. Specifically, revolution means the rising up of the Vietnamese people against foreign aggression in the form of collective triumphs over colonialism and imperialism.
In the Phiêu authored đổi mới document on national culture written to
correspond with the economic component of the state's đổi mới policies,
national culture is defined as "a front." Phiêu continues: "Building and
developing culture is a long-term cause of revolution, which requires
strong revolutionary will." This is not just an ode to a past achievement:
there seems to be an understanding on the part of the state that it believes
(even decades later) that the intersection of nationalism and revolution
shapes national culture (Marr 1995, 1984). This trajectory of national culture is useful for officials because the government continues to publicly
assert that there is a war occurring in Vietnam today, that of negative
foreign influence affecting Vietnam's unique and unalterable political-
economic ideals.

In his book *Fragments of the Present*, Taylor discusses the complex
chains of causation in the "erosion" of Vietnamese culture in the đổi mới
era (Taylor 2001: 129). The outcomes of these chains, which could also be
considered characteristics of the contemporary attacks on Vietnamese
culture, are many. State officials, sensing the country was spiraling into a

"moral and cultural crisis" (127), have issued official decrees deriding "bad cultural products," gambling, drugs, theft, juvenile delinquency, fraud, smuggling, and corruption (127, 128). Government officials run the gamut in assigning culpability. They blame everyone from rogue border agents to private entrepreneurs. More broadly, they cite the failure of such quintessentially "Vietnamese" principles such as national integrity, spiritual and moral values, and "national essence" in allowing cultural depravity to seep into the country (127-132). Culturally "problematic" cadre members have been publicly disciplined and the state continues to campaign feverishly to return to the "original cultural and spiritual abilities of the people" (Phong Lê 1991: 17, cited in Taylor 2001: 131). The government's hierarchical management of culture in these quotes is clear, and they identify a number of negative outcomes of a cultural war, yet the question of the state's role in culture's formation is omitted. Of what benefit is it to the state to invoke "good" and "bad" culture in these ways? In the following sections I answer this question with particular attention paid to the processual nature of official national culture, a culture that is valuable because it is in a constant state of re-creation.

## STANDING BY CULTURE: THE ORIGINS OF VIETNAMESE CULTURE IN 1945

*The ascendance of revolution in the Vietnamese cultural canon*

The year 1945 is a year in which the tensions between the creation of Vietnamese national culture and culture's worth to the nascent ruling class as a political instrument came into sharp relief (see Marr 1995). This year includes these historically significant events for the Vietnamese nation: the withdrawal of Japanese occupying forces in Vietnam after V-J Day; the concurrent Vietnamese "August Revolution" of 1945 (*cách mạng tháng tám*); and Hồ Chỉ Minh's famous September 2, 1945, speech in Ba Đình Square in Hanoi that declared Vietnam's independence to an audience of thousands of people. At that critical juncture in Vietnam's history the country was "unified," a new Communist-led government had been established, and the prospects of a society about to rid itself of colonialism's ills finally seemed visible. The August Revolution ended up being a short-lived period of Vietnamese nationhood unburdened by external meddling but the impact this particular year had on the state continues to influence the lives of ordinary Vietnamese in innumerable ways today. August and September, 1945, sit at the zenith for the state's revolutionary cause(s) (Tonnesson 1991).

The gravity of the August Revolution in the state's language, however, belies intense internal debate over the future of Vietnam. For example, in September 1945, in Vietnam even the proper naming of the country was subject to feverish dispute (Goscha 1996: 93). Nationalism was at stake; was the new country to continue to use "An Nam" as the common (if perjorative) appellation despite its use by the French colonialists and its connection to China, roughly translated in Chinese as "Pacified South"?[1] And what of Việt Nam, a related designation with Chinese origins (Taylor 1983)? How should Vietnam's colonial past be vitiated without contaminating the ruling government's cultural ideals, ideals that are themselves expediently invented? What I want to elicit from these questions is that behind the seemingly iron-willed, timeless cultural resolutions of the Vietnamese government that is investigated below there exists some tremendous ambivalence and misgivings about just exactly what Vietnamese culture is, where it comes from, what traits Vietnamese culture rests on, and most importantly, how it should be framed to a population that it can be argued does not always enthusiastically submit to national programming methods surrounding appropriate and inappropriate forms of Vietnamese culture.

Pelley's work summarizes the state's anxiety over its commitment to national culture after independence and the disquieting position that commitment entailed (2002). August, 1945, had finally brought Vietnam independence from colonialism and a most pressing question arose: how do we define ourselves? Pelley's answer is one of base/superstructure inversion (Pelley 2002: 116). Long subscribers to Marxist-Leninist styles of thought (if not adherents to its substance (*ibid.*)), leaders of the newly ruling Indochinese Communist Party (ICP) and precursor to today's Communist Party gravitated toward a base-superstructure model where cultural pillars unique to Vietnam were to determine economic and political outcomes. This inverts the usual base-cultural superstructure model in which the economy shapes cultural outcomes. Pelley outlines a number of traits disputed by Communist leaders. "In some cases," she writes, culture "referred to literature" written in the classic Chinese (nôm) and/ or Romanized Vietnamese script (called quốc ngữ, or script of the national language) (Pelley 2002: 114). Deciding on one or the other was problematic for a state determined to define Vietnam as a nation free of outside influence. Both the Chinese and Romanized scripts are descendants of China and France, respectively. Quốc ngữ was developed by Portuguese missionaries in the 1500s and indoctrinated in the 1600s by French missionary Alexander de Rhodes. In the early twentieth century the French colonial government made the Romanized Vietnamese script the official alphabet of Vietnam, and this alphabet is in official and everyday use today. Decisions on which language and script to use reflected concerns over what Vietnamese culture "is" and what Vietnamese culture could be successfully harnessed to.

In other cases, national culture was to include the "rich oral traditions" among Vietnamese people, traditions that had in many cases not yet been recorded in writing (*ibid.*). The commitment of oral traditions to writing offered the ICP a way to unite informal narratives around the country to "official" definitions of national culture, but problems were again to arise. While Pelley does not describe any of these oral traditions in detail, one can presume by the preponderance and importance of Vietnamese sayings in daily life today that one can include idioms ranging from "chín người, mười ý" ("nine people, ten ideas) to "tam tòng, tứ đức" ("three followings, four moralities"[2]) to "nhất nam nhất hữu, thập nữ nhất vô" ("one son is more important than ten daughters") in the oral traditional canon. These idioms are concrete examples of Vietnam's linguistic ties to the Chinese language, further representing Vietnam's inextricable link to China and complicating the construction of Vietnamese national culture. Moreover, many oral traditions among Vietnam's ethnic groups do not prescribe gender inequalities and roles to the extent that "Vietnamese" oral traditions like the ones mentioned above do. Do these traditions accurately represent the citizens of Vietnam and their cultural values?

Pelley goes on to state that Vietnamese culture was explained by the members of the ICP in the burgeoning days of its rule as "customs, costume and dress, life-cycle rituals, and, more diffusely, the texture of daily life" (*ibid.*). The identification and categorization of customs throughout the country is a daunting enough task, and any attempt to categorize a set of customs as "Vietnamese culture" would necessarily include elements of colonial influence (especially if bourgeoisie customs were incorporated). Lastly, she writes, Vietnam's national culture encompasses "health, hygiene, physical fitness, literacy, and intellectual and affective sensibilities, such as confidence in science, enthusiasm for labor, and devotion to the party" (*ibid.*). Vietnam's borders contain a rich diversity of customs and styles of dress, to say nothing of the Confucian, Buddhist, Catholic, and alternative religions that dictate life-cycle rituals. Given these variables, and the precarious position of a new (nonelected) Communist government, a coherent definition of Vietnamese national culture produced by the ICP and accepted by the populace at large would appear impossible.

Yet those members of the early ruling class who identify a cultural base and economic superstructure to Vietnamese society create a *style* of national identification that staunchly commits to Vietnamese culture however broadly and contradictorily defined. With Vietnamese culture as the basis for Vietnamese society, Vietnamese culture can mean anything, can include characteristics as diverse as language and hygiene, and can be used as justification for whatever programs and purposes the government deems important. In this light Vietnamese national culture's instrumentation is vastly more valuable than the practices and meanings the state identifies as aspects of Vietnamese culture. With culture at the base of Vietnamese society, the ICP can convince the population that the ideas and values that form the backbone of their lives mimic the ideas and values of the newly formed government. The state's base-superstructure inversion is beneficial for the government because it serves to further dislocate Vietnamese citizens from access to the state's cultural milieu due to the Vietnamese citizenry's collective culture being incorporated into the societal base. A dislocation from definitions of national culture would seem to have corresponding effects on the separation of Vietnamese citizens from the government's political apparatus.

As has become the case with contemporary versions of culture today, culture in 1945 was devised by government architects in terms of revolution. Suffusing the Vietnamese cultural base with nearly everything deemed cultural in Vietnamese society is valuable for the regime because sooner or later Vietnamese culture becomes meaningless. Government leaders gradually introduced a discourse of revolution into the myriad cultural traits in the national canon. "Referring to the 'cultural revolution' in Vietnam," Pelley remarks on the transition to ICP leadership under Hồ Chí Minh, "scholars looked at the prescriptive and utilitarian dimensions of culture and devised strategies for creating and disseminating a new canon of culture that would contribute to the realization of revolutionary goals" (Pelley 2002: 114). Understood as both the primary medium and outcome of Vietnamese cultural ideals, revolution had to be rethought by the ICP after independence because revolution—or the act of rising up against foreign aggressors—had been accomplished. The ICP understood revolution to be a key factor in Vietnam's independence, and their role in that independence, so revolution could not be easily discarded. Revolutionary goals had to be restructured to fit the model of a Vietnamese/ Communist-led country with culture at its base. Connecting revolution to its ideological cousin, culture, was the second order of business for ICP leaders after drawing innumerable characteristics into the national culture lexicon.

ICP-managed Vietnamese culture was thus reordered according to revolutionary programming in two ways. In the first place, the cultural base of Vietnamese society, with customs such as ancestor worship, kinship practices, and ceremonies were gradually replaced with principles of revolution; and secondly, Vietnam's cultural chronology began with the ICP's organization in 1930. New words crept into the state's lexicon, replacing ideas with long-standing meaning to Vietnamese citizens: rituals became "tasks," customs became "solutions," practices became "responsibilities." To rationalize culture this way established the new leadership as the creators and arbiters of a programmatic form of Vietnamese culture. Pulling literature, oral traditions, rituals, dress, health, intellect, and science into the category of Vietnamese culture dissolved their meanings into a vague national cultural base, to be replaced with a reinvented culture helmed by revolution.

*Early Reform Era Concerns with Culture*

As will be shown below, the contemporary ruling class's rhetoric and policy documents authored by Vietnamese officials prove that the use and promotion of national culture is part and parcel of the đổi mới policies and the reform era in general. However, preceding pronouncements of Vietnam's cultural strength and associated cultural campaigns, which began in the late 1990s and early 2000s, the reform era was characterized early on by state worries over the loss of culture as a result of market expansion. According to government leaders, globalization's benefits to Vietnam—rapidly increasing jobs and wages, global trade opportunities, stronger currency value, the betterment of everyday life for many Vietnamese citizens, and more exposure on the global stage through foreign tourism, media attention, and potential World Trade Organization membership—were being offset by the erosion of national culture by external forces.

Vietnam's youth play a critical role in state worries over the detrimental effects of negative, foreign culture on the country's social fabric. Therefore, state sponsored youth organizations are the primary acceptable means for young Vietnamese to organize, and a major state-owned national newspaper *Tuổi Trẻ* (*Youth*) is seen as an appropriate outlet for young people to give voice to their opinions about the direction of the country. Arguing that relations between young people and the government are "complex, interactive, and subject to significant change" (Nguyen 2006: 329), Nguyen shows how young people, in contrast to other societies which singularly lament the decadence and immorality of youth, are considered by the state to be "in the vanguard of the process of nation-building" (2006: 330). This point is amplified by Thomas, who shows how youth mobilization in Hanoi's public spaces are fraught with, on the one hand, official concerns over appropriate public behavior and on the other encouragement for creating communities that serve pro-Vietnamese political propaganda (2001).

Philip Taylor highlights state worries over culture after market reform had first taken hold (2001). Officials, sensing the country was spiraling into a "moral and cultural crisis" (2001: 127), issued official decrees deriding "bad cultural products" such as gambling, drugs, theft, juvenile delinquency, fraud, smuggling, and corruption (2001: 127-128). A series of announcements highlighting negative culture solidified into a program that was adopted nationally and focused on ridding the country of "social evils" (tệ nạn xã hội). The campaign was instituted in the late 1990s and was a passionately announced if arbitrarily executed initiative to rid Vietnam of foreign negative cultural evils and readjust the country according to the state's ambiguous vision of traditional Vietnamese values. Importantly, Vietnamese values are less well defined in the social evils program than "bad cultural products" are, and as technological advancements have made their way into Vietnam the regime has expanded social evils to include hazards such as Internet pornography, Facebook, and democratic activist blogger sites.

Government officials run the gamut in assigning culpability for allowing foreign cultural ideologies to enter Vietnam, from rogue border agents and private entrepreneurs to foreign tourists and the Internet. More broadly, they cite the failure of such quintessentially yet vaguely defined Vietnamese principles such as national integrity, spiritual and moral values, and national essence in allowing cultural depravity to seep into the country (P. Taylor 2001: 127-132). The social evils program thus constitutes an important ideological umbrella that has colored and directed the management of the Vietnamese reform era. On the other side of the coin, the state has more recently mounted a cultural offensive by proclaiming, sharing, and protecting its own unique and special cultural discourses in the face of perceived foreign cultural aggression. It is to an overview of the official construction and promotion of Vietnamese culture that the chapter now turns.

*Directing revolution and national equity: The state's management of a cultural offensive*

The presentation of the regime's Vietnamese culture is now an important counterpoint to the liabilities associated with market reform policies and has been indoctrinated into policy itself. As mentioned earlier, the state's vision of Vietnamese culture is vaguely defined but it is generally characterized by and repetitively linked to the twin themes of revolution, which harks back to colonial and imperial incursions into Vietnam (and the protracted fight for national independence) and socialism, based on Vietnam's long-standing socialist principles. The two terms are relational, with national equity serving to paint a picture of national solidarity and Vietnamese revolution spurred on by the unique ability of the Vietnamese people to congeal in times of external assault on them. In general then, revolution and national equity are the twin pillars of a multifaceted and elastic campaign aimed at reinforcing and promoting the state's Vietnamese culture. They are also tools used in the social evils campaign to attack negative cultural ideals and reward those communities and businesses that live up to the state's cultural standards.

The state labels communities with a Vietnamese culture tag and state culture is now cemented materially and discursively throughout the country in a number of different ways. Moreover, the ubiquity of culture highlights culture's malleable value to the government. Visits to historical museums operated by the state throughout the country, for example, describe Vietnam's heritage in terms of its struggle and triumph over Chinese, French, Japanese, American, Khmer, and other outside aggressors. It is significant to note that some of these museums—most critically the War Remnant's Museum in Ho Chi Minh City and the "Hanoi Hilton" (Hoa Lo Prison) where the North Vietnamese government held American prisoners of war during the "American" or Vietnam War—are some of the most popular sites in the country visited by foreign tourists, a sign that the state views the struggle against outsiders to be an enduring one (and one it would like to see promoted to guests from overseas). Additionally, a frequent slogan on street corners, and emblazoned on billboards in the central squares of towns throughout Vietnam is "Việt Nam Muôn Năm," which literally means "Vietnam (for) a million years" and has long been used as a rallying cry to inspire and mobilize Vietnam's people against external threats.

The state also uses culture as a means to caution Vietnamese society against consumerism and the perils of individual wealth. Taylor's comments below suggest consumerism's unwelcome infringement on the successes of the đổi mới policies and on Vietnamese national culture more generally:

> At the time that the economic benefits of Vietnam's "open door" (mở cửa) policy were just becoming noticeable, in the early 1990s, this reform began to be linked to a perceived crisis in the country's cultural and artistic traditions. Among the adverse effects identified by concerned commentators of opening the nation's doors to the non-socialist world were a "cult of exotic taste," the dizzying pace of borrowing, the resurgence of a cultural inferiority complex and the emergence of consumerism. (P. Taylor 2003: 139)

For these "concerned commentators" (cited by P. Taylor as state officials) standard economic practices in Western society like borrowing and lending infringe on Vietnam's cultural traditions. Since members of the political ruling class cannot renege on their self-praise for the creation and implementation of đổi mới (because that would degrade the state's capacity to implement and oversee economic policy decisions in the future) they have chosen to externalize Vietnam's societal problems on to outside forces. Vietnamese individuals are seen as succumbing to, rather than contributing to, destructive cultural influences such as selfishness and consumerism. Government leadership blames the "vice of reverence for foreign countries" for a range of impure mentalities, illegal behaviors, the pervasiveness of "un-Vietnamese" cultural symbols, and a lust for Westernized products, respectively. As examples, Marr and Rosen cite common themes like selfishness, smuggling, the ubiquity of foreign advertising, and the increased interest in culturally deviant materials such as "Coca-Cola, Madonna, and Hollywood" (1999: 181). According to government officials, these examples arrive in Vietnam from the outside and have no local foundation, forcing Vietnamese cultural narratives into a defensive position strengthened by the ideals of revolution and socialism.

As this section has shown, the tension and management of state-in-spired cultural strengths and cultural erosions in the context of market reform have become centerpieces of official public discourse. Another facet of the government's rule is that its economic strength through state-owned enterprises and "private" business ownership is inextricably tied to its unchallenged political rule. Over the span of the đổi mới policies' existence, state oversight of the national economy has been nearly as important as the implementation of the policies themselves. The leader-ship congratulates itself as the creator of đổi mới policies and expounds frequently on the successes of đổi mới. In a recent speech, Party Secretary General Nông Đức Mạnh prefaced the achievements of the đổi mới poli-cies with a nod to official supervision: "Political stability is the most im-portant factor that will lead to improving the country's comprehensive renovation process in an effective and sustainable way" (*Vietnam News* 2010). Later in the speech Secretary General Mạnh stated that develop-ment and socioeconomic matters were related matters, "affirming that the country must maintain socio-political stability if it wants to devel-op . . . (and) development creates the foundations for stability" (*Vietnam News* 2010).

The ties between economic development and socioeconomic stability are crucial for the state to maintain its one-party leadership but the quote above also hints at the ways in which political stability allows for the reform conditions set by the government to continue to sustain economic growth. By extension, Mạnh's comments aim to silence criticism aimed at the state's capacity to rent-seek. In the next section I argue that concerns about the wearing away of culture mask the ruling class's own worry that a loosening of state control over the national economy and the enhanced pursuit of wealth by non-state actors will disrupt the state-owned enter-prises' (SOEs) economic viability and undermine their political com-mand. If đổi mới is an instrument designed to build the national econo-my, how is national culture used to make sure the growth (or at least the maintenance) of the state-owned economic sector continues to be served by its political leadership? The next section evaluates this question using state-authored cultural policies.

## CULTURE THE STATE'S WAY: NATIONAL POLICY DIRECTIVES
## AND FOREIGN CRITIQUES

The cultural policy document translated below has been explained to me by government officials during fieldwork conducted in Ho Chi Minh City as the distinctly cultural component of the reform era policy package, which also includes economic and political directives. Entitled "The Res-olution of the Fifth Conference of the Party's Central Executive Board (session VIII) on Building and Developing an Advanced Vietnamese Culture, Which Is Typical of National Character," it was written in the run up to the Ninth National Party Congress in early 2001 by then–Vietnam Secretary General Lê Khả Phiêu, who as secretary general held the most powerful political position in Vietnam between 1997-2001. Secretary General Phiêu was subsequently ousted following the session but the document he authored was revised sporadically between 2001 and August, 2005. Upon inquiring about the government's cultural policies to officials on the Ho Chi Minh City tourism board, this was the document they provided me and said that it can answer all of my questions about Vietnamese and foreign culture in the reform era. The document I received was a hard-copy version and one was also published online. The document is 7,800 words long and the state's website stated that the publication was first published online on August 18, 2005. The document was available online on the state's website (under the national culture subheading) until the end of 2007.

The policy statements concern state authority over culture and the daily cultural battles among Vietnamese citizens, battles which are waged on production lines, in store fronts, and in the daily lives of people throughout the country. In no uncertain terms the official language from the leadership in Hanoi posits a Vietnamese culture predetermined to shape the country's current and future socioeconomic development plans. In sharp contrast to the global neoliberal economy, where governments withdraw from direct ownership and regulation of the economy, the state affirms that the transformation and strength of the Vietnamese economy has been possible because of Vietnamese culture, with direction and leadership from government officials. Official, state-led supervision and a cautious course of action—or proceeding differently (or more culturally) than Western and neoliberal models of growth when integrating into the global economy—benefits the state's desire to perpetuate its one-party rule and maintain the state's market share through its state–owned and private businesses.

What emerges from this cultural policy documentation is a repetitive cadence that centers on the now familiar lines of argument regarding what belongs in Vietnamese culture and more specifically what is to be left out. Representing culture as a "front," Secretary General Phiêu praises the virtues of a strong national culture based on revolution and national equity and triumph. However, Phiêu warns that Vietnamese people must never let up on their revolutionary ideals because to do so will weaken national culture. Therefore, revolution is a sustained feature of Vietnamese development. He writes that "building and developing culture is a long-term cause of revolution, which requires strong revolutionary will, cautiousness and patience" (8). Thus, there are in equal measures praise for the strength of state-sponsored Vietnamese culture through revolution and warnings against easing off of Vietnam's unique revolutionary spirit. Moreover, the cultural ideals of revolutionary struggle and equity after independence have a long historical legacy that further legitimizes their power and necessity during periods of Vietnamese transition. The opening paragraph states in part:

> Thanks to thousands of years of creative labor and of Vietnamese people communities' unyielding struggles for the sake of the nation, Vietnamese culture has come into being as it is nowadays. It can be said that Vietnamese culture has sharpened Vietnamese soul and spirit, thus brightening the nation's glorious history. In the age of Ho Chi Minh, Vietnamese culture, with the appropriate and creative policy of our Party, continues to be promoted, thus mainly contributing to our great victories in the struggle for national liberation and in the construction of socialism. (1)

The policy document thus focuses on Vietnamese culture's illumination through state leadership and the consistent use of revolution as a tool in beating back foreign attacks.

In another section of the policy, entitled "About the Reality of our Culture: The Achievements," culture arises from artistic representations of struggle: "In literature and art, creative activities have had new developments. Inspired by our revolution, wars of resistance and innovation, new valuable works of art have been created" (2). Here the terrain of revolutionary struggle is instilled by a Vietnamese culture that is illustrated through cultural artifacts like art. The kinds of art most likely to be considered state archetypes of Vietnamese national culture are paintings, like "portrayals of historic events or illustrious war heroes" (P. Taylor 2001: 109). They depict "legendary battles against Chinese invaders and . . . soldiers preparing to fight the enemy" (*ibid.*). Violent depictions of "us" versus "them" reinforce the revolutionary side of Vietnamese culture. Other acceptable artistic renderings portray the docile, determined spirit of Vietnamese farmers toiling in rice paddies, tending livestock, and using Vietnam's rich water bodies for replenishment and cleaning (P. Taylor 2001: 114). These representations of Vietnam are directly related to national equity and solidarity because they depict the sentiment that the Vietnamese cultural hearth and source of honest work and a peaceful, family-oriented existence resides in the countryside, while chaos, foreignness, depravity, and a decidedly un-Vietnamese way of life is apparent in the country's cities. But these passages also hint more broadly at what kinds of art are tolerated: that which is Vietnamese and not foreign, that which is not produced for a mass global audience, and that which is produced by Vietnamese artistic labels and promoters. Since the state defines, controls, and owns the artistic production and distribution channels in Vietnam, continued economic dominance of the artistic industry seems to be a component of the government's cultural directives.

As representations of Vietnamese resistance and equality, artistic expressions speak back to Vietnamese culture as a grounded verification of historical struggle and, contradictorily, tranquility and unity (N. Taylor 2001). From these examples of artistic production and the opening lines of the cultural policy package we can see that state-supported Vietnamese artists have the agency to facilitate the cultural ideal of revolution as well as depict rural-inspired tranquility. The contradiction between a violent and serene vision of culture is never reconciled because the tension reflects culture's malleability and, more specifically, its instrumentality to the state: revolution and equitability provide the state with a platform both to reward Vietnamese artists for their revolutionary accomplishments and to offer the prospect of a peaceful and equitable national society. That the latter is never fully attainable is of course based on the other side of an expedient cultural canon that reflects an enduring sense that the country is under attack by foreign powers. Additionally, "artist" is a sufficiently general category of cultural producer that the state can include and exclude individuals, organizations, and corporations on an ambiguous basis because of the vague nature of the term.

Culture-based artistry also facilitates more than the fluidity of the national Vietnamese culture and the promotion of state-sector artistic products. The state's cultural policies are a means to redress discrepancies between elderly imaginations of culture and young people's perceived ambivalence toward a state-led culture through an endorsement of a revolutionary type of artistic expression that can appeal to all age groups. After the state exuberates over art as a tool for the continuation of the revolutionary cause, the policy's wording goes on to tie historical art to young artists' revolutionary training. The policy explains,

> Most of the writers and artists have been trained as well as challenged in the reality of revolution. They are, therefore, experienced and patriotic. They still keep their virtue and determination to devote their creations to the public as well as maintain their role of being both soldiers and artists. Some artists and writers, despite being of old age, still pursue their creative careers while the young generation has taken great effort to look for something new. (2)

Troublesome, negative cultural trends on the part of Vietnam's young people are mollified by relating their artistic progress to elderly revolutionaries' work on behalf of the state. Additionally, the state gives young people artistic space to build "something new" while confining true artistry to Vietnamese revolution (and secondarily to a place-based serenity), depicted as it has been through warscapes ranging from border wars with China to long battles with the United States. Importantly, Western media is a frequent source of derision by the state and sometimes barred from being legally distributed in Vietnam. Therefore, stressing Vietnam's independent revolutionary spirit in the arts draws the country toward state-sponsored and approved arts and media outlets and pulls it away from Western cultural-economic and media products.

Indeed, revolutionary art has become a dominant product of Vietnamese material culture in the reform era. The state's cultural resolution seeks to broaden the scope of the Vietnamese cultural battle by identifying foreign countries' negative cultural baggage. A selection from the document has this to say on the subject of cultural damage:

> The vice of reverence for foreign countries and disregard for national cultural values, the selfish individualism, etc. . . . are doing harm to our fine customs. Cases are due to money and fame . . . Corruption and smuggling are increasing. Drugs, prostitution and other social evils are on the rise. Superstition is still quite popular. (3)

This passage functions for the state on two levels. First, Phiêu seems hesitant to directly equate foreign influence with degrading cultural mores. The passage works to a more subtle extent than previous calls to negatively categorize foreign culture. It is likely that the state recognizes that direct confrontation and dismissal of foreign culture and its products has the potential to adversely affect economic exchange, thereby treading lightly around cultural exchange. To proceed in an antagonistic way toward foreign culture also risks drawing the ire of the state's many investors who facilitate international cultural production. "The vice of reverence for foreign countries" allows this document a basis to couple foreign cultural products with the more philosophical vagaries associated with foreign cultural thought. But the decree, in its introductory remarks about "the vice of reverence and disregard for national cultural values," clearly suggests that everything from drugs and prostitution to individualism and fame fall under the banner of foreign culture.

In a related passage, the policy explains the tension between the Vietnamese market and negative culture this way: "Free market and international integration, despite their enormous positive effects, reveal their flip side, which negatively influence our people's ideology, morality and way of living." What this passage indicates is a desire on the part of the state to effectively manage the contradictions it sees arising out of the global economy: for example, supervising the betterment of Vietnamese society through gradual increases in access to capital and cautioning against this global capital's negative undertones. For some state officials it seems foreign culture isn't only a part of the transaction cost with other countries; foreign culture exists in foreign currency itself. This instills an air of caution to every encounter Vietnamese people are to have with foreign money or outside inventory and presumes that Vietnamese are aware of the difference between internal and external transactions and Vietnamese goods and foreign products. And in its association of foreign culture with some of the harmful features of the đổi mới economy, the state's cultural policies further orient Vietnam to acquiesce to its power by explicitly defining Vietnam's chronology based on a government built roadmap, drawing attention to its leadership throughout this progress and keeping the outside world separate from Vietnam in times of both war and peace.

The excerpts of the cultural policies underlined in this section high-light the state's realization of power through its ideal of Vietnamese culture. In invoking Vietnamese culture to consist of both the agency of the state and of Vietnamese people the government can use Vietnamese culture for a variety of purposes. For example, the cultural policies can exalt the usefulness of Vietnamese culture in the work of Vietnamese artists, which tacitly divorces state leadership from the construction of Vietnamese culture. The state can also regulate its version of Vietnamese culture. It segments Vietnamese citizenship based on artwork: it can condemn artists with "deviant" aspirations and laud those who serve a never-ending revolution. The state can also raise culture to a level above the practices of individuals, transferring it into a beacon guiding society as a whole.

It seems clear that much is to be accomplished in these passages, but perhaps the overarching point to come from the idea of Vietnamese culture is a certain political-economic bent that speaks both to the state's own ideological course and its economic intentions. Art is permissible only if it is cultural; that is, if it depicts revolution or serenity. This approach allows the state to monitor any art or innovation that it deems contradictory to these pillars, which includes entire sectors of the technology, media, and leisure economies. The position opens the door (and keeps it ajar) to insert its own enterprises into these profitable and rapidly developing sectors and reap the financial rewards that come from rent-seeking. Individualism and selfishness are not tenets of Vietnamese culture, so anything that isn't community-based will harm the country and should not be allowed to operate in Vietnam. Entrepreneurship would seem to be discouraged under this line of reasoning as individual profit-seeking motivations eat away at the socialist character of the Vietnamese people. Private, non-state firms, small businesses, and foreign-operated companies can therefore be targeted for violating the official cultural policies, to say nothing of the limits and strict regulations on private enterprise growth a critique of individualism provides the state. If Vietnamese covet foreign countries, they by extension covet outsiders's way of life. The government's cultural policies orient Vietnamese people toward Vietnamese products, Vietnamese-owned companies, and Vietnam's unique socialist inspired economic growth model, each of which benefit the businesses operated by state officials, state organizations, and government departments.

The reform era has confronted Vietnam's leadership with a number of challenges to its economic and political rule, and culture seems a useful tool in facing these challenges. As indicated by its cultural policies, the Vietnamese state has created a binary between Vietnamese and foreign that favors the sanctioned management of the political economy over any external model or inclusive of any foreign characteristics. Vietnamese national culture is resourceful precisely because it has been designed and executed with a deliberate malleability, a culture that despite the best efforts of the state to project as stable and resilient is in effect in constant flux, unfolding in reaction to new threats to its authority and goals.

## CONCLUSION

This chapter has outlined the ways in which the state constructs and uses Vietnamese culture as a tool in nation-building and as an expedient weapon of sorts against foreign aggressors. These aggressors come in many forms, and today their onslaught on national culture continues unabated. The state's national culture used to ward off foreign cultures confirms, idealizes, and positions further political decisions through revolutionary representations of the nation. And yet the counterbalance of an equitable and peaceful Vietnamese populace also serves official purposes. If Vietnam is an equitable culture, then the state can invent selfish, individualistic, and free market oriented foreign enemies that upset Vietnam's peace and reinforce the binary of insider/outsider once again.

But the analysis above extends the argument from a simple cultural exercise in the confirmation of statehood and legitimacy to demonstrate how culture is useful in the command of state economic rule. The reform era cultural policies show political rule and economic authority are intertwined to such an extent that it is difficult to separate them in analysis. Culture is used to keep state governance and the state-owned economy fused together as Vietnam transforms from a command economy to a socialist-inspired market economy, but it is also a tool employed to assert state rule over the Vietnamese political economy by blurring the boundaries between the Vietnamese market and national politics.

As a final point, the cultural policies of the reform era show that the state, in its communications with its citizens, has little interest in following a neoliberal development model espoused by Western lending organizations, certain development practitioners, and most leaders of the democratic Western world. If neoliberalism has become the "common-sense way many of us interpret, live in, and understand the world" as Harvey argues (2005: 3), an arena where "liberating individual entrepreneurial freedoms" is critical to the economic policies of governments around the world (Harvey 2005: 2), then the Vietnamese state has taken a decidedly strong stance against the agenda of the neoliberal marketplace. Although the Vietnamese marketplace has been opened to foreign investment, the cultural policies make clear that contesting the existing neoliberal economic model is paramount to Vietnamese society. In Asia, geographers critical of a neoliberal model of governance often implicate national governments in the adoption (Lee, Kim, and Wainwright 2010, Springer 2009b) and adaptation (Harvey 2005: 120) of neoliberalism. For the state, a free market that rewards entrepreneurship and individual prosperity is a trap set by foreign interlocutors interested in exploiting the Vietnamese economy and also damaging something integral and eternal to Vietnamese society: Vietnamese national culture.

Perhaps the more consequential question to ask with regard to the state's goals is this: What about the đổi mới policy package makes it seem as though the Vietnamese state has any interest in fully integrating into the global economy through "typical" neoliberal measures? Decreasing SOEs, reducing state services and market protections, encouraging investment and loans from a variety of sources (public and private, foreign and domestic), and exposing its national economy and its citizens to the peaks and valleys of unregulated economic development seem to have an insignificant role in Vietnam's reforms. For those interested in the implementation and reach of neoliberalism in postsocialist and Communist countries, the Vietnamese case study illustrates that contesting neoliberalism is not only a localized project among non-state actors: organizations interested in making their communities more economically prosperous or even more equitable by resisting neoliberal hegemony can find parallels in the rhetoric of the Vietnamese government's market liberalization program. However, just because the state opposes neoliberal thought and practice does not mean that it is accepting of an equitable and socialist-based society. A lesson to be drawn from the cultural policies is that even if neoliberalism is not accepted as a theory of national "political economic practices" (Harvey 2005: 2) then the alternative may not by default be a more just, superior, or even adequate alternative to neoliberalism. The Vietnamese state has created a reform-minded economy in which the cultural discourses of equitability, caution, and community play a role in drawing attention away from the state's predatory economic actions, actions which create solvency for SOEs and perhaps challenge the viability of private, non-state businesses. The production of national culture is expedient to the state because it can communicate cultural ideals to Vietnamese citizens who are sympathetic to the struggle against foreign aggression and the fight for national liberation but who may not buy into the government's ownership of a large chunk of the country's economic pie.

For Harvey, "Neoliberalization has in effect swept across the world like a vast tidal wave of institutional reform and discursive adjustment . . . (where) no place can claim total immunity (with the exception of a few states such as North Korea)" (2005: 145). Instead of showing how Vietnam has been pulled under the "vast tidal wave" of the neoliberal global economy, a closer inspection of Vietnamese reforms provides evidence of the government's refusal to submit to the inevitability of neoliberalization and the corresponding loss of political and economic control that comes with opening up the national economy to globalization. Thus, the more interesting exploratory question to pose with regard to cultural expediency and the Vietnamese political economy is not to ask how the Vietnamese political economy will be stifled by the state's restraints, but how the Vietnamese state and other postsocialist and Communist governments such as China will decide to manage and use national culture when it confronts new challenges to its leadership.

## NOTES

1. An Nam is the shortened name of *"An Nam quốc vương,"* which translates in Vietnamese and Mandarin to "King of the Pacified South" (Goscha 1996: 96).

2. "Tam tòng, tứ đức" or "three followings, four moralities" refers to a Vietnamese wife's responsibilities to her family and her husband's family after marriage. The three followings are: follow her parents at home, follow her husband after marriage, and follow her son after her husband dies. The four moralities are: housework (like cooking), female behavior and housekeeping, her behavior with outsiders, and faithfulness to her family and to her role as a daughter-in-law.

# FOUR

## State–Non-State Coordination in the Ho Chi Minh City Tourism Industry

This chapter evaluates the rise of non-state entrepreneurial opportunities in tourism during the reform era in Vietnam. The evaluation extends arguments made in the introductory chapter by critiquing the classic entrepreneurial city model advocated by David Harvey (1989) and others. The activities of many of the Ho Chi Minh City tourism industry entrepreneurs blur the lines that constitute "public" from "private," a division usually enforced by urban scholars in order to build a critique of the normative activities of the public (governance) and private sectors (profit-seeking). The division falsely distinguishes the activities of the public and private sectors into neat, distinct categories. This chapter offers an alternative picture of entrepreneurial activities that emphasizes the movement of firms and actors between traditional public and private categories. Moreover, it illustrates that the "murky" and "highly contentious" nature (Kerkvliet 2001: 239-240, also see Leshkowich 2008) of Ho Chi Minh City state-society relationships better depicts entrepreneurial practices than outlining whether or not (and to what extent) public officials and private investors are providing social services and lining their pockets, respectively.

The Ho Chi Minh City government—and in this chapter's case the tourism arm of the government—can be said to conduct business in a rapacious, competitive manner while at the same time continuing to have the means to regulate the local marketplace through policy initiatives. The government has long operated very successful businesses in the state and non-state tourism sectors (most importantly through the Saigontourist suite of businesses), confusing the public-private divide and presupposing Ho Chi Minh City as an entrepreneurial city. Ho Chi Minh City's non-state citizenry also pursues their own entrepreneurial endeavors and have been in competition with Vietnam's state-owned enterprises (SOEs) since before Vietnam's market reforms were introduced (Freeman 1996). Reinforced in this section is the thesis developed at the outset of the book: the relationship between the state and non-state sectors is more than a competitive one and in the Ho Chi Minh City tourism industry, for example, firms share business contacts and tourism routes, establish relationships built on reciprocity and trust, and barter their economic knowledges in order to gain consumers for their own businesses. This interaction complicates a "typical" entrepreneurial city's existing dimensions and introduces the importance of taking inventory of non-Western urban business practices through the lens of the hybrid cultural-economy.

The chapter begins by noting that in the conventional entrepreneurial city the power distribution among the public-private alliances favors the public sector. I adjust this unequal balance by presenting the influence of the non-state tourism sector in Ho Chi Minh City on initiatives in the local state sector. Relationships in Vietnam have historically shown their ability to transcend public-private distinctions, a point I raise in the subsequent section. The bulk of this chapter demonstrates how the public-private relationship plays out in the Ho Chi Minh City tourism industry, with an emphasis on non-state/private influence. Tourism has been targeted as a primary sector charged with "selling" Vietnam, and with Vietnam now serving thirty-five million domestic tourists per year (Vietnam National Administration of Tourism 2014) and surpassing seven million foreign visitors in 2013 (*ibid.*), the Ho Chi Minh City tourism sector provides a distinctive lens into the intersection of entrepreneurialism, coordination, and the marketing of Vietnam.

## UNEQUAL RELATIONS? THE FALSE FAVORITISM OF THE PUBLIC SECTOR IN URBAN ENTREPRENEURIALISM

The public-private division in much of the literature on the entrepreneurial city presumes a distinction between the state and the private sector, their roles in urbanization, and their command of political authority and capital, respectively. It favors the public sector over the private sector in making decisions about public-private ventures and presumes that urban state political influence compensates for its inability to act as the main funding machine for city growth. Relatedly, the model presumes that the ability of the private sector to finance projects in an urban setting is a weaker form of power than political influence is. This normative distinction between activities hampers the logic of the entrepreneurial city by assuming narrow governance practices of the urban state and perpetuating a private sector that has a singular interest in pursuing economic gain. Indeed, it is argued that city officials now have a "direct role" in the economic welfare of the city (Harvey 1989: 5) by assisting private interests in the speculative process of project financing. Entrepreneurial city managers, it is claimed, are charged with luring businesses with tax incentives, loans, and grants, forming relationships with private businesses, and conducting cheerleading and outreach programs to attract capital. "Urban governance has . . . become much more oriented to the provision of a "good business climate" and to the construction of all sorts of lures to bring capital into town" (Harvey 1989: 11).

There is an overriding sense of both opportunity and panic in entrepreneurial cities as the viability of Western city governments is now closely tied to the fluctuations of the marketplace rather than to the welfare of their urban citizenry. A good business climate must be implemented that proffers a safe, vibrant, and welcoming urban community that is equipped to respond to capital's entrance into the market. Political maneuvering is ruled by "improvements," with the local economy to be constantly stimulated by innovative inputs, like new cultural projects (such as sports stadiums, waterfront parks, and the like), and a consumerist urban environment has now become synonymous with an entrepreneurially successful city. The conclusion to be drawn is that the dramatic reduction of state funds allocated for cities and the increased mobility of capital have caused a shift in governance practices. Entrepreneurialism, previously seen as the domain of the private sector, is now characterized by the dominance of the urban state in making "good" political and economic (that is, commercially profitable and popular with citizens) decisions.

Though the presence of a universal public-private "alliance" in entrepreneurial city schemes is regularly invoked (McCann 2013, McCann and Ward 2011, Bezmez 2008, Hall and Hubbard 1998), alliances are usually heavily weighted toward the urban state rather than the private sector (though see McFarlane 2011 for an exception to this). In their now-classic geographical text on the subject of entrepreneurial cities, Hall and Hubbard write that "despite the seeming prominence of local business representatives in the new urban politics, it is clear that the 'voice' of the business community is still carefully circumscribed by both the central and local government, with the power often attributed to the private sector in urban coalitions frequently more apparent than real" (1998: 11). In an article by Wu and Zhang that recounts entrepreneurial city theorizing as it relates to Guangzhou and Hangzhou, China's, strategies for urban transformation, the authors discuss a series of strategic plans created by the governments of these cities in order to maintain their elite status in the national government and gain favors from the Chinese Communist Party. In their analysis these governments are "more than a business partner with non-government actors" (Wu and Zhang 2007: 717) because "remaking the city (is) the impetus for achieving political goals" (*ibid.*). Chinese cities like Guangzhou and Hangzhou are being remade in order for private actors to attain political favors from government officials. And yet the opposite has not been proven true: there is little about the ways in which officials turn over their political or economic goals (or even their decision-making) to the demands of private industry.

While the totality of this work has significant merits, evidence from Ho Chi Minh City illustrates that it is inadequate to posit a normative argument that conceptually separates public governance from private enterprise, or state agency and non-state financial backing. Moreover, the lines of influence and power distribution among the two are constantly being realigned, malleable in their functionality and better understood in relation to the everyday ties and challenges that arise among and between state and non-state actors rather than their reflection of formal rules and regulations. In Ho Chi Minh City any discussion about how the government *should* function must be weighed against how its entrepreneurial activities *carry out* speculative measures in conjunction with non-state actors. Moreover, what sort of analysis would result from an entrepreneurial city form of (non-Western) governance in which non-state firms and the decisions they make to inform local state practices are the institutions under analysis?

## ENTRENCHED AMBIGUITIES: RELATIONSHIPS BETWEEN THE STATE AND NON-STATE IN HO CHI MINH CITY

The relational aspects of the state–non-state alliance have a deep historical legacy in Vietnam but the relationship does not play out uniformly historically throughout the country. The forms entrepreneurship take, in other words, vary greatly according to the differences between rural and urban livelihoods, one's relationship to the government, education and training backgrounds, kinship ties, gender, and other influences. For example, in one of Kerkvliet's analyses of state-society relations prior to and leading up to the reunification of Vietnam in 1975 (see Kerkvliet and Porter 1995, Kerkvliet 2005, 2003, 2001), he describes "sneaky contracts" (*khoán chui*) set up by small-scale villagers in northern Vietnam (Kerkvliet 2001: 260). These villagers were supposed to be farming in village cooperatives with private plots officially "unauthorized" by the state (Kerkvliet 2001: 260). However, raising livestock was transformed into a profitable business as households were "contracted" by local political leaders to do the work decreed for cooperatives (Kerkvliet 2001: 260). In cases such as these village government leaders would—based on their kinship ties to villagers—often turn a blind eye to these arrangements.

Indeed, diverting attention from unauthorized businesses and activities is a long-standing strategy in business dealings throughout Vietnam. Moreover, it has longevity in tourism activities in Ho Chi Minh City as non-state entrepreneurs seek a quick, efficient means of accomplishing their goals. Local officials seem to have their own intentions behind these charges. City leaders, officials, and local police put themselves at risk by ignoring "illegal" businesses and by accepting money but the rewards for a speculative approach to local oversight can be rich indeed: acquiesance to one's elder relatives' financial needs brings rewards in the afterlife (Harms 2012), ingratiation to a spouse's family does the same, and supplemental income provides for one's family when formal wages will not. These arrangements are born out of negotiation, trust, risk, and reward; in other words, they are quintessentially entrepreneurial and parallel registers of the urban cultural-economy. These examples touch on the breadth and embeddedness of coordinative arrangements undertaken by state and non-state actors in Vietnam and represent the ways in which the entrepreneurial city unfolds using arrangements that cannot be reduced solely to political and/or economic opportunities. Importantly, the state's own entrepreneurial intentions have been imperative to (but not a sole driver of) "the persistent and extensive problems of getting villagers to behave as good collective members" (Kerkvliet 2001: 261). In other words, it is not always in the best interest of the state for society to follow its rules.

To cite an urban example of this point, David Koh argues against popular understandings of contemporary Vietnamese governance that tends to equate "communism" with "repression" and "authoritarianism" (2001a, also see 2001b). These stereotypes are based on the state's own pronouncements of its top-down authority, created and maintained in order to institute and implement decisions encompassing the entirety of economic and social life in Vietnam. However, the overwhelming sense of domination and hierarchy that many commentators associate with the state government masks the "negotiation and mutual influence between state and society in Vietnam, especially in everyday activities that are socio-economic in nature" (Koh 2001a: 281). Using a case study of karaoke bars in Ho Chi Minh City and Hanoi, Koh demonstrates this point by showing how the state and non-state use each other to continue to reap financial rewards despite the execution of a national social evils program aimed at curbing depravities occurring at these places. Karaoke bars, usually fronts for prostitution, gambling, and drugs, are run by canny non-state businesspeople who "often establish patron-client relationships at both the upper and lower levels of local administration as well as all specialist agencies, including the police, the Bureau (of Prevention of Social Evils), and the State Inspectorate" (Koh 2001a: 291). These relationships transcend national initiatives such as the social evils program. And in light of their weight in cities like Ho Chi Minh City and Hanoi, these connections frequently drive local policy decisions. As Koh states, "when people evade, struggle, and negotiate around party-state regimes, they often use the local administration as an important ally" (2001a: 283). Under these circumstances, it seems unlikely that local administrators would neglect entrenched informal relationships in favor of broad and perhaps fleeting national policy programs like the social evils campaign.

Freeman (1996)—writing about the informal, non-state sector from the French colonial period beginning in the late 1800s—makes a convincing case that "petty craft and marketing enterprises were an important feature of the regional economy" (1996: 187) early in Saigon's colonial era. He cites examples through to the Communist takeover of South Vietnam in 1975 when national leaders were too occupied with enforcing economic regulations over large and medium-sized private businesses in Ho Chi Minh City to be bothered with informal enterprise (1996: 188). "From the outset," Freeman states, "the communist economic policies of the South were inconsistent and ineffective" (1996: 188). The erratic nature of policy implementation and enforcement provided the informal non-state enterprise sector with the outlet it needed to perpetuate the trade of small-scale consumer goods and services. When the government did meddle in informal activities (often draining small non-state reserves through bribe and tax payments), the sector showed its resilience by appealing to hội (hui in Chinese), or credit circles that include overseas remittances, neighbor and relative "mattress banks," Chinese investors, and the like (1996: 191). While I do not mean to diminish the local state's role in Ho Chi Minh City's rapid economic growth, my intention is to point out the historical strength of the non-state sector in continuing to accumulate capital under colonialism, during the post-reunification command economy, and through reform.

In Ho Chi Minh City both the public and private, or the state and the non-state, are motivated by entrepreneurial goals. Instead of thinking solely about the ways in which the Ho Chi Minh City government rent-seeks under đổi mới, or emphasizing the capacity of the non-state sector to engage in the pursuit of economic prosperity in light of đổi mới, Ho Chi Minh City is a lens into the ways in which the divisions between the state and non-state economies may be more blurry today than ever before. Given this point, how do the state and non-state negotiate entrepreneurship to harness capital?

## LOCAL ENTREPRENEURIALISM IN ACTION

### *Market liberalization? The bumpy road following reform*

Reflecting the uneven, fluctuating nature of state–non-state relationships in Ho Chi Minh City, one non-state tourism executive explained his first, challenging interactions with Ho Chi Minh City officials. His company was created during the summer of 1992, in the opening days of the đổi mới reforms. Because at the time Todd—as an overseas Vietnamese—could not operate his own company in Vietnam the company was officially owned and listed under his aunt's name, since she had remained in Vietnam during the 1970s and 1980s. His company is therefore designated as a Vietnamese-owned, non-state company. Todd expected his entrepreneurial skills honed in the Western world would serve him well in Ho Chi Minh City. Instead, he expressed shock as he relayed to me how the local government interacted with his company at the time:

> My brother, who remained in the United States, helped our company cultivate numerous Vietnamese-American contacts to fund our business. We also had a long list of Vietnamese living in California, as well as other Americans, and they were interested in traveling to Vietnam. The Saigon government must've heard about our contact list, because one day they came in with the police and confiscated all of our computers, all of our (accounting) books, and all of our contacts lists. There was nothing we could do! They called it a compulsory "audit" (*kiểm tra*) to make sure we were in compliance with đổi mới. They said all companies must go through this process, even though I knew from friends that this was a lie. They said if we didn't give up our customer information they would shut us down immediately. About three weeks later we got most of our paperwork back, and we immediately began calling all of our contacts to warn them about security breaches, identity theft, something like that. A lot of them told us that other companies from Saigon were trying to sell them tours, sell them pieces of companies, and were even pushing them to fund new tourism companies! I lost so much business from that situation because they made copies of all of our clients' personal information. The worst thing was that they asked my clients what they were paying for trips to Vietnam and offered them a lower price for the same one!

This case shows that the local Ho Chi Minh City government—now decentralized from the national government, faced with burgeoning non-state competition, and encouraged to engage in its own business activities without the promise of perpetual solvency from Hanoi—had turned to aggression in its dealings with competitors. This is a neglected form of urban state entrepreneurialism yet it is a trenchant facet of local officials' attempts to contain market losses as a result of the liberalization of the urban economy. Todd's frustrated diatribe against the state illustrates that the state's preferred mode of coordination with the non-state in the early days of đổi mới was executed by force and theft. This story reflects the frustration often felt by Ho Chi Minh City non-state small business operators at the time who came to believe that the strong arming tactics of the local state demonstrate city officials' "greed and paranoia" at the changing dynamics of non-state competition in post–đổi mới Vietnam (Leshkowich 2008: 17). Adding insult to injury, Todd noted that at the time he had to pay "fees" to the office of the Vietnam National Administration of Tourism (VNAT) in order to continue operations. Payoffs like this do not hold a place in most narratives of entrepreneurial cities, where the actions of both the public and private sectors are to coordinate in order to profit from investment capital, not to destroy private businesses.

As mentioned previously, the market reforms arrived in conjunction with the decision in 1990 to assign provincial status to the major cities of Ho Chi Minh City, Hanoi, and Haiphong (and later Danang and Can Tho), giving these cities' governments greater autonomy to act entrepreneurially than ever before. This meant that officials in these cities have the same policy, decision-making, and voting authority as leaders in the other provinces of Vietnam. In rewriting the provincial map of Vietnam, national authorities in Hanoi designated cities as the primary drivers for Vietnamese development. When I asked Todd how he knew the police and auditors were from the local police, rather than the district or ward police, he told me that the city police wore different uniforms than the district police. His informal discussions with other newly minted entrepreneurs who were also visited by officials confirmed that his circumstance with the local authorities was not an isolated incident. Moreover, Todd noted that he had met a few of the auditors at meetings set up by the local officials with new non-state entrepreneurs. These interactions posit that local Ho Chi Minh City officials—perhaps wary of a more level playing field and worried about the viability of their own tourism businesses in light of their new autonomy from the central state—worked in coordination with local police in bullying new non-state businesses.

Despite the predatory practices of the state at the outset of the policy reforms it seems from interviews with Todd (as well as from Leshkowich's analysis [2008]) that both the state and non-state exhibit characteristics of urban entrepreneurialism. Many non-state entrepreneurs were catalyzed by the market reforms to establish new businesses throughout the city. However, they lacked useful contacts in the urban government who could expedite their needs and allow them to operate without meddling, they hadn't yet staked out a strong and respected market niche in the tourism market, and weren't necessarily tapped into the extensive network of informal lending that has come to characterize much of Ho Chi Minh City's economy (Truitt 2013). These new market entrants were exploited by the local state for its own ends. Thus the amount of financial risk incurred by the non-state during this time of "new change" in the city was clear and much of it was experienced through the state–non-state relationship. Should non-state actors such as Todd openly resist the audit and fees exacted from the government at the time it is highly unlikely his business would have survived. These acts represented the costs of operating a non-state business in Ho Chi Minh City in the early years of market reform. But as Todd noted later in the interview, one of the results that arose out of paying fees, being forced into audits, and attending meetings was that employees of his company began developing relationships with local government contacts. A formation of this kind of public-private/state–non-state relationship does not neatly fit into the existing dimensions of the entrepreneurial city. And now, when Todd needs a favor from the government, like a permit to travel or bring guests to a politically unstable region in the country, or special dispensation for travelers with expired visas, he need only invoke the years in which authorities preyed on his business and he says that officials usually agree to his periodic requests.

In these ways Todd and other non-state tourism operators like him, while not necessarily changing local policies, are proving that local entrepreneurial policies are not stable. They are not based solely on the characteristics of advanced capitalist urban entrepreneurship but are evolutionary ways of doing business in Ho Chi Minh City. These nascent, difficult, yet productive encounters between the state and non-state were the seeds by which a new form of entrepreneurialism was to emerge.

*Joint venture operations in Ho Chi Minh City: Blurred boundaries and shifting roles*

Todd's initially challenging interactions with Ho Chi Minh City officials in the early days of the national market reforms gave way in the late 1990s to a more coordinative and less predatory relationship between the state and non-state. An example of these new dimensions comes from a French-owned joint venture tourism company that began operations in the mid-1990s. Mark, who started as a tour guide with the company in 1999 and eventually rose to become its director of marketing, conveyed the fuzziness of the joint ventures operating in Ho Chi Minh City today through an example of the evolution of his own company. Officially, he said, a foreign-owned company who wishes to promote and market tourism offerings within Vietnam must partner with an SOE or government-backed organization. Otherwise foreign-owned companies are free to market to countries outside Vietnam, but not in Vietnam itself. Additionally, foreign-owned companies cannot own their own transportation, purchase land or real estate, or hire their own tour guides (they must be hired as independent contractors).

The decision to partner with a local Ho Chi Minh City university, as Mark's company did, came because the owners felt that a joint venture provided a much easier path through bureaucratic red tape and various legal trappings, which Mark said has proven true. His company also desired to promote tourism offerings to the burgeoning middle class in Vietnam that has become a sizable market niche in its own right (see Nguyen-Marshall, Drummond, and Bélanger [2012], and more will be said about this group in chapter 6). The university was the public entity in the entrepreneurial relationship and it was charged with coordinating with the French-owned private company. Mark explained that "ours was the first joint venture between a European company and a Vietnamese group, which was impressive, and still is." It is impressive because as

Kate Lloyd has written Saigontourist—still the SOE tourism industry be-
hemoth in Ho Chi Minh City—has been openly critical of joint ventures,
claiming that they create "'unfavorable conditions' and 'unfair competition' by having superior facilities, overseas booking networks and preferential airlines" (2004: 205). As a foreign-owned tourism company executive named Paul remarked when I asked him why his company hasn't
chosen to partner with a local governmental unit, he stated,

> The government never has any money. That's the biggest reason (why
> we don't establish a joint venture). They are always asking us to give
> money for them to go on roadshows, to promote Vietnam around the
> world. Life could be made very difficult for us if we didn't give them
> money for this stuff, so we obviously do. We've been receptive to a
> joint venture in the past, but it hasn't worked out. We'd love to be fully
> licensed as a joint venture, but that isn't going to happen for a while.

For this company, the decision to establish a joint venture seems to be a
difficult and tricky decision with a high degree of risk attached. Whereas
Mark's company made the decision to establish a joint venture, and the
relationship has been a thriving one, Paul decided that the level of risk
and potential for loss of profits were too high. Under traditional understandings of the coordinative urban entrepreneurial relationship the public sector is seen as the chief decision-maker in the relationship. However,
in the case of the Ho Chi Minh City tourism industry it is the non-state
sector that weighs the pros and cons of coordination and only partners if
conditions seem optimal and investment and opportunities are expected
to be shared.

That said, there is less of a separation between the state and non-state
in both of these cases than one may imagine. Paul's company still sporadically pays into a fund allowing city officials to travel around the world
promoting Ho Chi Minh City and Vietnam. There are "fact-sharing"
meetings organized by Ho Chi Minh City officials that are required
should foreign-owned companies wish to continue operations. The importance of these meetings is not lost on executives such as Mark and
Paul who are aware of the barriers to entry, market restrictions, and rent-
seeking that remains even after the establishment of market reform and
corresponding relaxation of Vietnam's protectionist policies and practices.

Critically, Mark struggled when pressed to name the local Ho Chi
Minh City university his company has forged a joint venture with. "We
are associated with a university in Saigon, but I am unsure of the exact
name," he admitted. On the other hand the university's leaders "have a
say in the everyday operations of the company." To add another wrinkle
of ambiguity to Mark's description of the inner workings of this joint
venture he repeatedly said that one of the reasons his company is successful, and has continued to grow since the 1990s, is because "they (the

university partner) don't know anything about tourism, which is a good thing."

A viable conclusion drawn from these comments is that the official terms of the relationship between the state and non-state are vague and consistently up for discussion. Indeed, Mark bookended our discussion about the joint-venture relationship by saying that "sometimes the Vietnamese partners attempt to take over the (foreign-owned) business, but that hasn't been the case with us at all. Actually, once a joint venture becomes successful the Vietnamese company usually wants to take over." This comment suggests joint ventures are shared partnerships in name only, with a 50-50 stake in the decision-making and profit-sharing of the joint venture an illusion. Paul's remarks suggest something similar in referring to his company's relative wealth compared to the Vietnamese government. When I pressed Mark about how profits were distributed between the two entities, he was similarly vague. "They join us for meetings sometimes, and I know we spend a lot of money sending Tết (Vietnamese Lunar New Year) gifts to each member, but how money changes hands during the year, I don't know."

While this statement may seem questionable in light of Mark's status as a "higher-up" in the company, it points to two broad conclusions. The first is that Mark understands how profits and decision-making are shared but he is reluctant to explain them. This is certainly plausible in light of Western notions of business ethical standards and their application to or disuse in a Vietnamese case study. He may have felt I wouldn't understand or would disagree ethically with the financial dealings between the two groups. On the other hand (and the conclusion I choose to draw) is that Mark cannot adequately explain the parameters of the relationship and so he leaves them unclear. In traditional analyses of the entrepreneurial city the public-private relationship is, by virtue of the private sector's absence, dictated and driven by the public sector. The dynamics of this Ho Chi Minh City example are ill-suited to easy clarification under traditional terms of urban entrepreneurialism.

This is not to say that the relationship between Mark's company and their university partner has not settled into one of mutual understanding, because Mark acknowledges that the university group has decision-making capacity, yet it seems clear they generally choose not to exercise it. That the relationship has flourished for almost two decades proves that both groups find it useful. Within the broad terms Mark describes, however, there seems much room for maneuvering by both the state and non-state. The exact dimensions of the entrepreneurial affiliation between the two groups seem less important than the value each group draws from it. And the university's stake in a private enterprise makes it clear that the normative differences between state governance and private entrepreneurial profit-seeking are unfit for the Ho Chi Minh City tourism economy example. Moreover, in Paul's company's case—from fact-sharing meetings to sporadic payouts for local officials—the lines demarcating where the state's role in governing and the non-state's role in facilitating business is indistinct.

*Working together: New market niches forged by state–non-state coordination*

Vinh would consider himself to be an entrepreneur. At the age of twenty-three he left his home in Ben Tre (about eighty kilometers south of Ho Chi Minh City) and settled in the city to find work. He soon became fluent in English (the de facto language of the tourism industry) and then decided to pay a visit to a well-known locally owned, non-state tour company in Ho Chi Minh City to enlist his services as a guide. He quickly rose up the corporate ladder at his company due to his entrepreneurial scheming. He described to me in detail one of his most successful initiatives to date. One of the most common routes Vinh accompanies tourists on as a tour guide is a day trip from Ho Chi Minh City to the Mekong Delta region. The traditional centerpiece of this trip is a boat ride down the Mekong River so tourists can take in the floating markets and local life in the countryside. Many companies, including Vinh's, offer this trip and tourist boats are regularly seen jockeying for the best views and stops down the river during peak season. The boat trip, which comes after lunch, happens to pass by Vinh's hometown of Ben Tre. Eager to show off his accomplishments in the English language and his ability to manage a large group of foreigners to his family, on one occasion he spontaneously directed the tour bus driver to meet the group at his family's home instead of at the normal ending point for the company's scheduled boat trip. The result of this rendezvous was unexpected but overwhelmingly successful. Instead of his family being entertained by his English abilities and the eccentric behavior of foreign tourists Vinh found that the foreign tourists devoured the nooks and crannies of his boyhood home and his family's hospitality (which in his mind were both unexceptional). On the way back to Ho Chi Minh City Vinh was struck by the tourists' consistent referral of his home as the "real" or authentic Vietnam and his tips that day reflected the tourist group's enthusiasm. Vinh then relayed to me the rest of the story:

> I think that tourists want something different. I decided to make my home a place where they can come and enjoy traditional Vietnamese food, drink, and real culture, which is about the family here. I told my mom and sister to make food and clean the house. I asked my dad and two brothers to plant some coconut, banana, and mango trees near the house. One day it will be a farm too, and we can sell coconut candy, coffee, and other things for my family.

I accompanied Vinh on one of his tourist trips to the Mekong Delta (and without the tourists' or his company's knowledge, to his family's home).

Approximately midway through the boat trip there had been no mention of Vinh's hometown, his family, or even his home. Without warning a motorboat sped up beside the tourist boat and a young man climbed onto our boat. Vinh then calmly said,

> My friends, this is my brother Hung. He is twenty-four years old. He has just come to our boat from my family's home, which is just a few kilometers away. It is the home I was born in and grew up in. I want to offer you two choices for the rest of your day with me. You can choose to continue the regular tour and meet the bus back where we started. My brother will take you on the regular tour with him. But since we are so close to my family's home, I want to take you there. There we can eat coconut, drink some rice wine, visit with my relatives, and you can see another part of Vietnam that is not available to most people. At my home you can be a part of the real Vietnamese culture. You will be able to arrive back in Ho Chi Minh City at the normal time.

The abruptness of Vinh's brother's entrance—itself interpreted as a spontaneous act by the tourist group—suggests a staged atmosphere to Vinh and Hung's performance. His brother arrived on cue as a personification of a new, inviting type of culture introduced to the group. On the trip I participated in there were no tourists who were inclined to follow the "stock" tour and I later learned that tourists virtually never choose to continue the regular trip provided by Vinh's brother. The tour group— with guests from the United States, France, Australia, Israel, the United Kingdom, and Canada—collectively seemed to be entranced by the prospect of visiting a real Vietnamese home and their enthusiasm was bolstered by the timing of Vinh's brother Hung's visit: the tour group had already established a relationship with their tour guide, and this new, unexpected visit seemed to be a logical extension of the progress of that relationship.

Vinh's family home is the connection between his livelihood as a tour guide and his family's financial needs. On the trip I was on his family had set up makeshift stands selling products from coconut trees (like wine and candy). Vinh explained to the group that Vietnamese culture dictates that unmarried sisters, mothers, grandmothers, and grandfathers are to be taken care of by their offspring. Having now met his family and seen their small, old home, and having been his family's favored guests there, Vinh said, could his new friends spare some extra money in tips for his family when they arrived back in Ho Chi Minh City? The response on the part of the tourists was a complex sense of awkwardness, pity, joy, appreciation, and philanthropic spirit. The large amount of tips at the end of day proved Vinh's detour had worked as an entrepreneurial endeavor and he told me later that his family makes a lot of additional money selling coconut products to tourists.

Vinh's side trip to his family home in Ben Tre conveys duplicity, feigns sincerity, fabricates living conditions in order to tug at heartstrings, and manufactures a specific idea of culture in order to amass capital. But narratives such as this story has equals among other Ho Chi Minh City non-state tour guides and firms. The following week I met with Vinh and a number of his tour guide friends who work for non-state firms in the city for a gathering at a local restaurant. I joined them because I wanted to fact-check statements made by tour guides I had interviewed the previous month and to cross-reference information about the local tourism industry I had heard about or read in the news. Many tour guides regularly meet to take the temperature of the local tourism industry, discuss new market players (and players that have folded), trade insider information, swap stories, and share their professional and personal lives with each other. The tour guides greeted me and I began to document their discussions. What arose from the meeting was that many of the tour guides were appropriating their family homes, whether they were homes of distant or close relatives, whether comparatively well-off or poor, and each spun stories similar to Vinh's to (foreign) tourists. Additionally the promotion, invitation, and financial winnings from the visits, far from being insubordinate activities, occur with each firm's blessing. Tour guides took turns relaying favored strategies for recruiting tourists to the family home, parlaying cultural ideologies of the home into saleable entities, "hiring" family members to produce new cultural products of the home, and sharing other tall tales involving the economic fleecing of gullible tourists. Sitting with the group of guides was a quiet gentleman who, like me, was listening to the proceedings closely. He hardly said anything, only rarely interjecting to clarify a point. He also seemed to be conducting research on the tourism industry. After the meeting I introduced myself to him. He introduced himself as Liem, an executive for an SOE who was planning on incorporating "home" tourist trips into his own company's program soon.

This meeting shows the complicity of non-state actors in furnishing the local entrepreneurial government with seemingly proprietary, lucrative competitive knowledge and it highlights this knowledge's absorption by a local state representative of a mega-SOE tourism operation. The saleable home becomes an institution that further blurs the lines dividing the practices and regulations of SOE firms in Ho Chi Minh City from the alternative practices of their non-state tourism firm counterparts. The "home as tourist site" example collapses the concrete definitions of state officials/SOE executives and non-state tourism actors who represent the public and private of the traditional entrepreneurial city model in cities throughout the world. The marketing of the Vietnamese home, then, becomes a symbol of the ambiguities by which local actors and their institutions practice their version of urban entrepreneurialism; one that is negotiated, coordinative, and most importantly, exists as a mediated relationship between the local state and non-state tourism operators. More generally it proves that cities like Ho Chi Minh City do not submit to the conventional understandings of urban entrepreneurship.

# FIVE

## Commodifying Memory

### *Touring Warscapes in South Vietnam*

The reform period has seen the Ho Chi Minh City private tourism industry attune its tour offerings to the segment of consumer who fought and/or participated in the "American" war (Le 2014, Butler and Suntikul 2012, Alneng 2002). Sensing a lucrative market niche in offering tours of painful memory sites, yet aware of the potential for further emotional and psychological harm caused to tourists with ties to these sites, private firms now create specific tours based on consumers' tour desires which weave together memory spaces of pain, loss, euphoria, and regret. These spaces carry names which, when invoked, conjure up this collage of remembrances. They can be Dak To, or Hue, or Loc Ninh, or Saigon. Tour operators have before them a challenge to create and package an aura of remembrance that can be consumed by foreign tourists. Memories of pain and the places that are imbued with these memories are subjected to tourist commodification in the same ways as other sites. But the commodification of these sites, as I show below, does not deprive these places of their past. Rather, commodification and memory work together through the tourism experience. This chapter analyzes two specialized tours of the Vietnam-American war through the lens of culture and memory. Culture and memory have special merit when employed together because they provide tourism hosts in Vietnam who consider themselves to be part of a distinct Vietnamese "culture" the ability to symbolize their culture by evoking the past. It is through these evocations that tourism hosts rescript the present with specific discourses and material representations of history. In Vietnam this is an especially fruitful exercise in both the material and discursive senses because many of today's tourist spaces—full of merriment, alluring narratives, and fiscal exchange—were

67

once painful spaces marked by death, starvation, loss, and further degrees of pain. What also emerges in an overview of culture and memory's contested meanings is the innovative ways tourism operators make use of these tensions in the sale of place for consumers. I argue that meanings of culture and "memory," though frequently intersected in explanations of *commemorative* symbols and war landscapes (see Baird and Le Billon 2012, Kwon 2012, Malarney 2011), have in large part not yet been explained in the context of *commodified* symbols and landscapes. It seems that although culture and its material landscapes can be memorialized with regard to war their utility as mediators of monetary exchange is often omitted in the literature (though see Butler and Suntikul [2012] and Schwenkel [2006] for examples of the uses of memory in tourism practices). The argument has been made that memorialized places and the cultures they represent can be considered sites of contention between the state's version of the past and everyday spatial memories (Muzaini 2014, Muzaini and Yeoh 2005), but the deliberate deployment of culture and memory in war landscapes for the explicit purposes of consumptive activities also deserves critical attention.

The two tours discussed below are conducted by private firms in south Vietnam and originate out of Ho Chi Minh City. The first involves an effort to locate the approximate vicinity of the death of a member of a foreign (and usually American) military regime during the Vietnam War and then taking relatives of the deceased to the site where their loved one passed away. The second tour is conducted to mark the crash of one of the Operation Babylift airplanes, in April, 1975, at a site about five kilometers outside of Ho Chi Minh City (Sachs 2011).

These tours create a productive tension for private tourism firms, that of a "dead" past and an animated present. This two-pronged form of dead past and progressive future is attractive for tourist consumers who have already been conditioned to memorialize Vietnam through visual imageries inscribed by darkness, pain, and death. That there was a Vietnam War, and that the war is a source of still current contradictory emotions for the foreigners that served in Vietnam is a well-established manner of consciousness in the Western world. Primarily, of course, these feelings have been appropriated in American motion pictures of the war (Alneng 2002). In this sense tourists are no strangers to the commodification of the war, a fact not lost on Ho Chi Minh City's private tourism firms.

This chapter stretches the practices of tours in their responsibility to condition memories of the past in a consumptive light. Although both tours contain rehabilitative elements for tour operators and tourists, the central concepts exercised here are commodification and consumption. As ephemeral or economically self-serving as this interpretation of the war landscape may seem (and thus lacking in any sort of substantive meaning, such as "coming to grips" with pain and memories, or using the landscape to purge or symbolize pain and ugly memories), its presentation sheds light on the innovative or entrepreneurial transformation of pain into a culturally strategic place like a war site.

## Transforming memory into a commodity

In a well-known edited volume on memory in Vietnam, H-T. H. Tai writes that "if it were not for the (equally) ubiquitous symbols of the global economy such as Coca-Cola bottles, karaoke bars, golf courses, and computers, Vietnam would appear to be living in the past" (2001: 1). While an important addition to Vietnam's links to the past during the reform era, Tai's comments dismiss the preponderance of global products in Vietnam and instead lead the reader down the memory lanes of contemporary Vietnam. Though some commentators focus their analyses on the impact of globalization and the broad suite of offerings sold in Vietnam after the introduction of đổi mới (e.g., Truitt 2013, Schwenkel and Leshkowich 2012, Drummond and Thomas 2003), Tai argues that memory plays a critical role in state-society relations. For Tai, the spoils of global integration correlate to advantages for nongovernmental actors who wish to explore their own personalized accounts of memory. She writes, "the decline of High Socialist orthodoxy, relative prosperity, and prolonged peace have encouraged other actors besides the state to try to occupy the space of memory" (2001: 1).

What is interesting about these passages is that Tai allows for local actors to constitute memory spaces but regards the products of the global economy as a backdrop to these affectations. In the first place, illegitimating as "ubiquitous" global economic brands in the Vietnamese economic landscape disregards their localized appropriation. Peter Jackson refutes those who argue that the world is already "globalized," preferring to conceive of a "globalizing" world with local permutations of global phenomenon (2004: 165). In support of this thesis he states that no "single society (can) claim to provide the 'authentic' source of meaning for any particular commodity or cultural form" (Jackson 2004: 166). Tourism, as a dimension of the global product economy like Coca-Cola or computers, is captured as a particular kind of brand in various environments and scales for appropriation. Pierre Nora, whose legacy in the arena of memory studies is "considerable" (Legg 2005: 482) believes in the "movement toward democratization and mass culture on a global scale" (Nora 1989: 7). His premise is not in keeping with recent work that (following Jackson) analyzes the local arrangement of global products such as tourism (see Ormond 2013, Su 2011). Although Nora's work on memory is entertained in this chapter, his explanation of global mass culture and memory deserves refinement.

In the second place, if Vietnam is currently experiencing a watershed moment in its integration into the global economy through đổi mới, why does memory continue to be conceptually separated from the commodities that memory often represents? Moreover, why is memory rendered approachable by non-state actors in this "open door" era under Tai's reading while the injections of global commodities such as Coca-Cola into Vietnam are abstracted from their local adaptations? One answer to these questions could be the conceptual bias that memory, and specifically memories of the Vietnam War, receive over consumption and commodification. But a primary question usually left out of conversations in Vietnamese tourism studies is how Vietnamese hosts—tourism companies, tour operators, and tour guides—guide memory so that it can be commodified *and* have an emotional impact. An appropriate balance must be levied: enticing tourists through stark indicators of war—which are already embedded into their memories—coupled with an overall sense that tourists can derive pleasure out of these violent objects of interest.

In tourism practices, no person, place, or thing is left external to consumption, including landscapes of war and pain. To be sure, such sites are subject to processes of "sacralization" (Lennon and Foley 2010, Muzaini, Teo, and Yeoh 2007, Rojek and Urry 1997) when they are injected with symbolic value, highly articulated expectations, and graphic and narrative representations. But one should not delink the consumptive tendencies of tourists from their desires to experience and engage with a painful memory site. Instead an understanding that war landscapes, while certainly in processes of sacralization, are shot through with consumptive desires reinterprets both the sites themselves and the practices of the tourism actors who shape their commodification.

## LANDSCAPES OF PAIN, REVISITED AS COMMODITIES

*Background to the tours*

Tien Giang province is located about sixty-five kilometers south of Ho Chi Minh City. Its capital is My Tho, a large port city that lies on the northernmost branch of the Mekong River. Provincial citizens work primarily in agriculture, producing rice, fish (like catfish), shellfish, fish sauce, and fruit. It also has some large rubber fields, a legacy of the French occupation. During the Vietnam-American war the province served as a major site of United States military operations, and indeed the first base to be constructed in this part of Vietnam was called Dong Tam (in English, "Uniting Hearts"), about eight kilometers west of My Tho. It was a joint Army/Navy military complex that was constructed in 1967 under the guidance of General William Westmoreland, who also named it. A major reason the U.S. military decided to build a large base there was because of the influence of National Liberation Front (NLF, colloquially and pejoratively known as "Viet Cong") insurgents throughout South Vietnam and that part of the area specifically (Biggs 2012). There were a number of thoughts regarding the makeup and goals of this group by the U.S. military, but one that was commonly agreed was that their operations were swaying popular local opinion against U.S. presence and therefore were dampening the prospect of democracy in the fledgling country of South Vietnam. As a result, there was much clandestine military activity and related casualties in 1967-1968 among both Viet Cong and American forces.

It is in this region where one private tourism company in Ho Chi Minh City conducts highly specialized and expensive tours aimed at locating the approximate site of the death of a foreign soldier in the U.S. military ("GI"). Using mapping software, conducting interviews with local residents, and analyzing archival records this tourism company aims to be able to bring foreign tourists who have lost loved ones in the war to the site of their family member's passing. These tours are offered to foreign guests who would like to pay homage to their family members, visit Vietnam, and come to grips with their loved one's death.

Another tragedy that occurred at the end of the war was a failed Operation Babylift flight that resulted in a deadly crash just after taking off from Saigon's international airport on April 4, 1975. Operation Babylift was a controversial decision made by then-U.S. president Gerald Ford in the waning days of the Vietnam War to sanction Vietnamese orphans to be transported ("evacuated") by airplane to Western countries such as the United States, Canada, and Australia, where the children were to lead ostensibly better lives in democratic nations. One of the first official flights of this operation crashed and resulted in one hundred thirty eight deaths, including one hundred twenty-seven orphans and numerous humanitarian volunteers, or over half of the plane's occupants. After takeoff the plane's rear doors flew open and the flight crew (U.S. Air Force pilots) turned the plane around in an attempt to return to Tan Son Nhat airport. The plane went down outside of the airport in a rice paddy (Peck-Barnes 2000). As of 2015, I am not aware of an official memorial at the site. Despite this enormous calamity the evacuations continued and by April 30, 1975 (the official ending date of the war), approximately two thousand six hundred orphans were taken out of Vietnam.[1]

Stories of these tour offerings were shared by two private tourism operators in Ho Chi Minh City; in the Đong Tam case, by the founder and president of a high-end private tourism company, named Hùng, and in the Operation Babylift case by an executive of a midrange tourism company named Sang. The following sections delve into each tour's details separately.

*Building tourism commodities out of painful memories in south Vietnam*

In the mid-1960s, during a search by the 9th Infantry Division in the U.S. Army for suspected NLF insurgents in the village of My Phuoc in South Vietnam, a young man named Tom stepped on a landmine and was killed. He left behind a wife and two children. Among other custom tours he arranges for foreign tourists, the one Hùng offers that locates the approximate spot of a loved one's passing and then takes the family to the site is (he says) his most popular. This involves a broad, diverse network of connections on his and his company's part. To locate the approximate location of someone like Tom's passing, Hùng's employees use data from his Vietnamese contacts and their U.S. counterparts who search year-round for bodies of Missing In Action (MIA) Vietnamese and Americans.[2] He also uses declassified records from the U.S. archives by sending his employees from his U.S. branch office to study them (he also claims he can access some of these documents online). Local Vietnamese employees seek out former and/or current residents of Tien Giang province to give voice to his statistical findings. He then sends a tour guide and one of his bus drivers to the approximate site to ask questions of its residents. He sometimes participates in trips like these, too, depending on the difficulty of the case and the level of involvement (and compensation) from his clients. Their questions are centered on: Did this battle or American death happen here, on this day, at this time, and did it involve Americans from Dong Tam? After Hùng validates his client's relative or friend's death in an approximate area, he has his employees send the location to the tourist. At this stage of the journey clients transform into tourists and pay for a site visit option separately. If they are interested in making a personal journey, Hùng has a suite of travel options available to them.

Hùng's tourism offering is interesting because of the way he repetitively describes Tom's family's experience as indicative of how his company weaves together commodification and memory at these painful sites. For him, there is no sacrilege in profiting from the pain of the past nor does "selling" the site weaken its memorial power for guests. Moreover, how Hùng selectively narrates his own memories of that particular experience in his explanation of the family's trip to visit the site of Tom's death adds another layer to the commodification-memory nexus.

He relays one particular story in this way. Tom's widow and her two grown children arrived in Ho Chi Minh City a few years ago and everyone (including Hùng) traveled to Tien Giang together. Hùng explained to me that the first day in Tiền Giang was exhausting for Tom's relatives. Due to time constraints the family could only stay for five days in Vietnam, and only two of those days would be in Tiền Giang. Sometimes, Hùng says, he can arrange for a meeting or a meal with the local residents, and he was able to organize something with Tom's family. In this family's case he was able to arrange a community dinner with local residents. About fifteen neighbors had gathered there that evening to eat (the combination of a party—provided free of charge by Hùng's company—and a family of foreigners attracted people from the village). As dinner started and Hùng welcomed everyone, a very elderly man became visibly uncomfortable, shaking and mumbling to himself. He pointed at Tom's sons, crying and with his voice rising. The visiting family was dumbstruck and sat uncomfortably awaiting a translation. Hùng froze. He told me that he asked himself, "should I translate what this man is saying?" He explained that he hesitatingly decided to and stated quietly, "this man says he planted the landmine that killed your father." The old man recognized the faces of Tom's sons because, as Hùng said to me, "everyone remembers the faces of the people you kill," and this elderly man recognized Tom's face in his sons'. After the initial disquiet at this shocking serendipity, the man hugged, wept, and ate with the family for the rest of the night. According to Hùng, Tom's family—while initially stunned and speechless at the disclosure—found that this discovery and subsequent meal with the community softened them to Vietnam, humanized their understandings and memories of the war, and allowed them some peace over the death of their father and husband. Hùng also proudly mentioned that they made an immediate donation to the Tiền Giang man's family after their initial visit. Now, the American family "has fallen in love with Vietnam" and comes back every year to Tiền Giang to visit and heal the wounds of the war with its residents. Hùng's company organizes the tour each year for the family.

Hùng has probably shared this story with me three or four times over the course of my fieldwork years in Vietnam even though he does not remember the elderly man from Tiền Giang's name, he does not remember Tom's last name, nor does he remember his family member's first names. He can't recall the name of the village in Tiền Giang where these events occurred and he does not clearly recollect which year Tom's family first arrived in Vietnam. His excuse for losing his memory regarding these details is that he is no longer a tour guide but an executive with many guests and accounts to consider. Their first visit was a while ago, he also always states, and the details aren't as important as the "truth" (sự thật) of the experience. Why then would Hùng relay this story to me numerous times? It is clear that for Hùng the specifics of the American family's first encounter with the site of their loved one's death are indeed dead, largely forgotten in the fuzziness of past economic transactions. What he emphasizes in our conversations are Tom's family's repetitive trips back to Tiền Giang, their philanthropy toward the community, and Tiền Giang's lack of infrastructure. These parts of the tourism experience filled Hùng with passion and he often mentioned to me that "the segment of tourist guest who comes to Vietnam to visit the site of their relative's passing ALWAYS comes back for a return visit and we are very happy to provide their accomodations and serve them."

It is of course obvious what aspect Hùng remembers from his relationship with the family. But it is imperative to analyze these acts of remembering in conjunction with what has been forgotten, because as Nora states memory "remains in permanent evolution, open to the dialectic of remembering and forgetting, vulnerable to manipulation and appropriation, susceptible to being long dormant and periodically revived" (Nora 1989: 8). We should not equate the process of remembering and forgetting as a zero-sum game with memory loss coming at the benefit of remembrance "gains" (see Muzaini 2015). Additionally, categorically separating the two in memory analysis distorts an accurate picture of their constitutive relationship. How then do we proceed analytically? Fruitful options include a deconstruction of the specificities of Hùng's language and bodily movements in his storytelling; how certain knowledges are created from the repetition of his narrative (i.e., the fantastical dimensions of tourism encounters or how dead bodies mediate knowledge in this area of tourism); or of how Hùng's remembrances relate to tourist's long-standing search for certain unique and exotic forms of authenticity (MacCannell 1989). Each have their intellectual merit, but each neglect both tourism as a consumptive activity that yields capital for its facilitators and culture as a "field of force" (Yúdice 2003) that drives the pursuit of capital.

It would also seem at the outset that Hùng's memories are a function of his long tenure in the Ho Chi Minh City tourism industry and thus a common or understandable casualty of time. But assigning benefits and weaknesses to Hùng's memory fails to take into account the performative aspects of his recollections. Hùng's memory classifies the past in specific terms: categories of necessity are constructed for the tourism marketplace, such as the history of his company, his family, and his professional evolution. But his memory also groups certain marketable moments from his life as a tour guide and company executive to authorize his work as legitimate, to convey his company's prowess and innovation, and to hint at his company's advantages in a competitive marketplace. He fleshes out a verbal marketing strategy from these personal and professional attributes, a kind of presentational pitch on behalf of him and his office. For Hùng this "selective" memory, I argue, is a charactertistic of his presentation of Vietnamese culture introduced purposefully in order to generate profit. If tourists can be enticed toward a certain destination then, as Britton's classic work on tourism argues, "tourists by and large are conditioned to look for the qualities associated with a cultural model, staged performance, or life-style representation" (Britton 1991: 455, and see Larsen and Urry 2011).

It was evident to me during our discussions about this particular tour that Hùng was posturing his company's innovative techniques against other tourism companies in Ho Chi Minh City. He is aware of my interaction with a variety of different tour operators throughout the city and he undoubtedly wishes to create a narrative by which I will remember his company amidst the cavalcade of other narratives I am exposed to. What he believes is that an original narrative within the context of an innovative tourism endeavor would solidify his company's place in my research. But there is more to his stories than simply a need to be recognized by a researcher like me. Hùng undeniably believes he understands the desires of the tourist guest. If tourists are conditioned to render familiar a certain model of staged performance in tourism experiences, then they are also prepared and indeed desire a glint of spontaneity or serendipity to these experiences. In the more traditional sense one can think of the ubiquity of audience participation throughout the world in comedy shows, operas, circus acts, etc. The cultural model Britton speaks of is permeable, but it does have limits. If a positive relationship with Tom's killer in the countryside was not the end result of the family's visit, if there was a fresh antagonism born between Vietnamese and Americans instead of a friendship then it is doubtful the story would be relayed to me, let alone repetitively. Since it didn't Hùng can control his remembrances and forgetfulness toward a collective memory that rehashes American memories of the war in a positive light. The spontaneity of this encounter becomes another trait in a staged performance, one that is rich with the possibilities of financial reward if it is marketed well to others. It is not as if Americans visiting contemporary Vietnam are unaware of the sentiment presented by the media and other popular vehicles that cultural dislocations between the United States and Vietnam were an important aspect of the failure of the United States in Vietnam during the war. This stereotype is carried through much of the southern Vietnamese tourism sector in the form of progovernment tourism sites like the War Remnant's Museum (Schwenkel 2009) and the Cu Chi Tunnels (Le 2014). However, it is also used as a vehicle to commodify healing on both sides of the war, as will be outlined in the next section.

*An opportunity for tourism? The tragedy and opportunity of Operation Babylift*

The lack of an official (or even unofficial) Operation Babylift memorial does not deter visits to the site by orphaned survivors of the Operation Babylift endeavor, relatives of the deceased, some veterans of the war, and other interested parties. Another tour operator named Sang has a relative monopoly on this package tour. He has spent the past few years arranging annual tours to the site of the crash. On the thirtieth anniversary of Operation Babylift in 2005 Sang organized a special tour in conjunction with World Airways, the private commercial and cargo air carrier that was contracted by the United States government to initialize the evacuations in 1975. The fortieth anniversary of the Fall of Saigon in 2015

is marked by another special tour that draws together survivors of the
Operation Babylift crash and overseas Vietnamese who were evacuated
during the action.

In explaining his company's role in the tour, Sang took a cool, business-like approach to the package he offers:

> Every year a woman from Denver, CO, brings over a group of Vietna-
> mese-Americans from the United States who were a part of Operation
> Babylift to visit the site. We arrange for a visit to an orphanage where
> many of them were housed (Phu My orphanage in Bình Thạnh dis-
> trict), and even meet with some of the old sisters that ran the orphan-
> age while they were there. I don't really know the Denver woman's
> background, except that she runs their tour. I do remember that the
> Denver "sister" was angry because she wanted privacy for the group.
> (Chuckles to himself.) Some of the people who lived near the crash site
> have remnants from the crash, like seats (from the plane) and so on. We
> (Sang's company) take them to these neighbors. Sometimes they will
> invite the guests to their homes to look at the remains of the crash. We
> of course pay for their food and give some money to the neighbors for
> their time.
>
> World Airways isn't really a commercial carrier, but it was their
> plane that went down in Saigon that day. World Airways brought over
> some orphans for two nights and three days on the thirtieth anniver-
> sary of the crash (2005) and paid for everyone to visit the site. There
> were a total of seventy people involved in that trip. They even met with
> the People's Committee! It was all done very well, they had red carpet
> to greet them at Tân Sơn Nhất Airport. I deal with someone from that
> airline in St. Louis or Atlanta, I cannot remember which city.

Sang's process of remembering and forgetting mirrors Hùng's. That he
doesn't recall his Denver associate's name and background seems remarkable given that Sang's company personally facilitates tours with Operation Babylift actors every year. But it can also be said that specific
names are often forgotten in the sheer amount of contacts Sang has as he
develops his business throughout the world. I want therefore to draw
attention to the comment that elicited the most emotion from him during
our conversation, the quiet laughter at the United States organizer's insistence that the tour to the Operation Babylift crash site be kept private. I
asked him about why he smirked at this request, and his face eased:

> Americans think very much about this site. When kids die it is impor-
> tant to everyone, but for us Vietnamese the tragedy was thirty years
> ago! We (Vietnamese) choose to have ghost celebrations for the chil-
> dren in private. But for you Americans the place is more important
> than the death itself! They would not allow me to take a video of the
> anniversary tour.

For Nora the term "nostalgia" has its genesis in the Greek term for a
painful longing (algia) to return home (nostos) (cited in Legg 2005: 285).

The term's etymology makes sense for Vietnamese-Americans whose life story begins by being abruptly uprooted from their home. It also makes sense for relatives of the adoptees, deceased flight crew, and volunteers who long to reconfigure their memories of the crash in place. The U.S. contingent that travels to the site every year in remembrance of the Operation Babylift tragedy would seem to epitomize Nora's nostalgia with an unrequited emptiness and long-standing hurt that can only be partially satiated through annual trips to the Operation Babylift site. And yet there is little nostalgic memory articulated in Sang's words about the tragedy, only a measured explanation of the components of the tour and some of the more unique aspects of tourist responses to the magnitude of their emotions. Sang situates the Operation Babylift crash in the past and dismisses the way that these tourists choose to cohabitate the crash space with their past. He vividly recalls some of the ways that he ushers tourists to consume the past, however: visits to Phu My orphanage, through local residents' hoarding of the plane's fragments, and the way he stresses visits to the surrounding homes in his explanations of the tours. Elements of the tour that have the possibility for monetary gain for Sang—most apparently in the form of certain meaning-making between tourists and the various sites that allows for them to consider long-term financial investments in memories of the Operation Babylift site—take precedence over other exchanges such as Sang's personal relationship to tourists, his understanding of their desire for privacy on their tours, or his and his family's historical ties to and implication in the war landscape. In this way Sang filters his business through the memories of the Operation Babylift tragedy. Memory thus has an expedient value for Sang.

What kind of expediency is at work in Sang's description of the Operation Babylift tour, and what is its worth to him and his business prospects? In the passage above he certainly seems to understand, if not relate to, the needs of American tourists to square their memories of the flight crash with the authentic site of the disaster. Sang has a grip on the notion that "re-presented landscapes offer Western tourists memories of a past that stabilize and authenticate not the past so much as the tourist's position within it" (Kennedy and Williams 2001: 151). It is not, in other words, Sang's positionality vis-à-vis the Operation Babylift memory that concerns him, it is his customers' memories. This transferal of value—from an internal, articulated memory of the Operation Babylift crash to a culturalized memory in a potentially consumptive environment—frames the site's expedient significance for tourism operators like Sang.

*Can Ho Chi Minh City's tourism operators perform the present and past at the same time?*

At first glance American tourists who visit Vietnam are confronted with the realization that their conceptions of Vietnam's past are dead.

Popular media representations of the Vietnam-American war stand in stark contrast to a population that presents visual cues that they are forging ahead with their economic lives. These clarifications give credence to the recurring statistics often shown in Western media outlets that joyfully exclaim measurable improvements to south Vietnamese lives (see Hayton [2010], for a discussion of Vietnam's explosive growth and Truitt [2013] and Luong [2009] who outline Ho Chi Minh City's development). Whether this is actually the case for south Vietnamese citizens is beside the point. Evidence exists in the visual landscape before them that south Vietnamese citizens are taking advantage of market openings to accumulate capital by nearly every means they have at their disposal. In Western consciousness money equals happiness, and we may also add that money provides a route to "move forward." This generalization can be validated by tourism studies that attempt to delve into the tourist consciousness, especially in studies where "authentic" tourism can only be experienced by visiting difficult-to-access places, thereby allowing only a certain segment upper-class consumer to enjoy and define their experiences as "genuine" (Cohen and Cohen 2012, Silverman 2012). Tourists often comment on the spirit of hard work and entrepreneurialism that seems to permeate contemporary Vietnamese society. These stereotypes prefigure a collective movement on the part of Vietnamese people to move past the horrific events that occurred during the war. Indeed, there are few clearly observable vestiges of the Vietnam-American war in the country aside from the sites of resistance promoted by the Vietnamese state and a few museums dedicated to this message. An inherent curiosity forms around tourists who visit south Vietnam that must be rectified by Vietnamese tourism operators whose economic livelihoods depend in part on the clear representation of the historical interaction between Americans and Vietnamese during the war. This interaction is part of the cultural model that makes American consumers (and other Westerners) feel a sense of familiarity to the staged tourist performance. Hùng's narrative of Tom's family and Sang's account of the Operation Babylift crash illuminate the past for consumers and reconcile the tension between a progressive and entrepreneurial present and forgotten past by formulating it in a consumptive context.

Tourists imagine history through visual and narrative representations of a past that resembles something familiar to them. Tourism operators such as Hùng and Sang understand that many American tourists have real memories of Vietnam without ever setting foot in the country. Touring Vietnam allows tourists to fulfill their desire to fill in gaps in their perspectives of certain memories already made meaningful to them prior to their visit. How to elucidate and reinforce existing memories of Vietnam for tourist consumption is the tour operator's task, and this task is made more difficult with the visible indicators of economic power like skyscrapers, malls, and billboards. These signs enliven Vietnam's economic landscape but do not lend themselves to the memorialization of war. Western tourists visiting south Vietnam are also keen to reimagine the war through these landscapes of pain without feeling encumbered by the familiar and uncomfortable trappings of tourism pomp and pushiness. In the case of Marks's family the re-creation of a war landscape, while certainly familiar, does not beg for monetary investment. It is up to tourism operators to consolidate memories into imaginations and make these imaginations clear amidst a rapidly expanding market economy. Hùng and Sang's narratives are a means to explore measures that bridge the memories of the past with visible indications of a fluid present in marketing their tourism itineraries to tourists.

Indeed, Kennedy and Williams provide an apt commentary to Hùng and Sang's exploits:

> The expertise of the tourism firms lies in their ability to coordinate the logistical aspects of their clients' international journeys, but that can only occur after those travelers have been enticed to the destination by the promise of some desirable experience. Thus tour operators pay close attention both to the sites that potential travelers might visit and to the literature that will familiarize them with those sites in advance. (Kennedy and Williams 2001: 144)

This chapter shows that tourism firms research and bracket U.S. tourist memories as consumable entities in order to follow their own economically minded pursuits. Representations of the Vietnam-American war are conduits for Western travels to south Vietnam. A certain segment of tourist consumer appropriates popular representations with their own painful memories of the war, and this effort distinguishes them from the backpackers, business investors, and "leisure" class who travel to Vietnam. In the case of both tours highlighted above, tourists' impetus for travel is the desire to shed light on their painful memories and complete fissures in their understandings of the site, Vietnam, and circumstances of their loved ones' deaths. It is up to tourism operators to be able to legitimate these painful past memories in a former nation (South Vietnam) where the current government actively discourages war memorialization such as cemeteries, memorials, battlefields, monuments, and plaques (Malarney 2011).

Private tourism operators assimilate foreign memories into their tourism packages to differentiate their business from other tourism competitors. Because many of these private tourism operators were in close contact with Americans during the Vietnamese-American war, it may be reasonable to consider their motivations to be built on desires beyond financial accumulation and company growth: feelings of sympathy, empathy, and commiseration are part of the overall cultural-economy. These emotions also may be catalysts for the creation of new tours. As mentioned earlier, many scholars writing on contemporary Vietnam cannot help themselves from venerating memory in its own right yet do not acknowledge the ways in which memories can be commodified without necessarily losing their meaningfulness as a site of pain or remembrance in the process. Meanings and memories of pain are not lost when sites are rescripted for tourists; they are rearranged to derive benefits for both the consumer and the producer. Their engineering of memory sites into unique tourist destinations demonstrates that no memory can be excluded from its value as a commodity.

## NOTES

1. One major criticism of Ford's decision revolved around whether or not the orphans were actually "orphaned" or not. In the aftermath of the operation numerous Vietnamese families explained that they were under the impression that the orphanages would care for their children while they were under varying degrees of peril, and that when the societal situation calmed down in south Vietnam these parents would be able to reclaim their children. See Sachs (2011), and Navarre (2004) for some mention of this.

2. The two United States Missing In Action organizations are the Defense Prisoner of War/Missing Personnel Office (DPMO) in Washington, DC, and the Joint POW/MIA Accounting Command (JPAC) located in Hawaii and Hanoi. Incidentally, these organizations also search for equipment, such as downed airplanes, and unexploded ordnance.

# SIX

## Domestic Tourism in Vietnam

*Disruptions of a Dialectic and a "Stereotypical" Response*

### INTRODUCTION

Since the establishment of its open door policies, Vietnam has seen a massive rise in tourism activity. While foreign visits receive more scholarly attention (see Suntikul, Butler, and Airey 2010; Suntikul, Airey, and Butler 2008), it is the domestic tourism market that has experienced higher growth rates. Recent data from the Vietnam National Administration of Tourism (VNAT) indicates that the domestic tourism market is approximately four times larger than the international tourism industry. Between 2007 and 2013, for example, domestic tourist trips have grown almost twofold, from 19,000,000 to 35,000,000 tourist trips. In the last year of available statistical data, domestic tourist trips grew by almost 8 percent (VNAT 2014).

This chapter concerns the substantial rise in Vietnamese domestic tourism and its consequences for the country's tourism industry. In outlining the relationship between Vietnamese tour guides and Vietnamese tourists, this chapter also addresses the changing face of Vietnamese identity as it unfolds through tourism. The đổi mới policies initially shaped the Vietnamese tourism industry by encouraging foreign tourists to visit the country. Vietnamese tour guides and other English-speaking Vietnamese service sector professionals supported these visitors. Domestic tourism in the late 1980s and early 1990s was scarce except for pilgrimage tourism and visiting family and friends (Singh 2009). At that time foreigners were known to be flush with money, to have a certain corporate acumen, and to be largely ignorant of Vietnamese society. Vietnamese nationals represented the other side of the coin: although economically poor and lacking in formal training, Vietnamese people were nonetheless able to fully understand the complexities of Vietnamese life and offer a singular perspective on the daily rhythms of its residents in ways that foreigners could not.

The maturation of the đổi mới period has recast the dialectic between foreign outsider and Vietnamese insider as it is articulated through the Vietnamese tourism industry. If the previous two chapters looked "outward," asking questions about how tourism services are produced for foreigners that link the past with the present under the specter of đổi mới, this chapter discusses the consequences for Vietnamese identity built on a stable, impenetrable culture in the open door period. The Vietnamese tourism industry is an ideal lens into changes in Vietnamese identity because it is through tourism that "Vietnameseness" has been presented to (foreign) tourists. It has been seen as a source of stability and usefulness for the tourism industry that showcases it to tourists. This form of Vietnamese identity follows the official visions of national culture: stable and eternal, resistant and equitable, and useful as a discursive instrument in the sale of Vietnam. But the changing face of Vietnamese consumerism—and the identities it engenders—means that the boundaries between insider and outsider are quickly breaking down.

In research conducted in Ho Chi Minh City since 2002, I have learned that "foreigners" (người nước ngoài) are often coveted for their spending power, compliance, and generosity, intrigue of Vietnamese socioeconomic character, and generally easy-going dispositions. The quintessential tourist consumer is the "người tây" (Western person), for s/he symbolizes wealth, status, openness, "outsideness," and a certain gullibility that is laden within these identities. However, "người tây" are now not the only tourists who consume Vietnamese culture. The dialectic that previously existed in Vietnam between foreign tourists and "insider" Vietnamese— between those who have the ability to tour Vietnam and who are in the business of presenting Vietnam to these actors—has collapsed. Trevor Barnes states that a dialectic is "defined as an opposition that propels change" (2006: 38) and dialectics have historically been employed as a method for analysis by Marxist scholars. However, because it is a "productive" method rather than a form of scientific verification (Barnes 2006: 37) it is increasingly being used in other aspects of the social sciences, including as a framework for identity-building.

With the dialectical oppositional categories of the foreign tourist outside and the national inside as the theoretical basis for my chapter I ask the following question: what happens to Vietnamese identities if the outside category of Westerner is already filled with identities driven primarily by leisure and consumerism? Recent years have seen dramatic changes in Vietnam's economic landscape, and Ho Chi Minh City is at the forefront of these changes, so it may be legitimate at least at the onset to retort, "why can't both Vietnamese and Western identities have a consumerist dimension to them?" The point that I hope to make in this chapter is that both do, but that they are substantially different in scope and tenor, with Vietnamese and other Asian tourists consuming from the inside and Westerners consuming from a vantage point outside Vietnam, causing friction and contradiction among tourism operators over the ideology and future of the quintessential tourist.

This chapter has two subsequent parts and a conclusion. The first is to extend my argument from chapter 3 concerning the state's presentation of Vietnamese culture as eternal and unchanging. By focusing its policies on the twin goals of external investment from "outside countries" and monitoring Vietnamese culture from the inside, the state underscores the idea that Vietnamese people will sustain their consumption habits amidst a growing economic sector but stable cultural environment. In reality, of course, this is not the case because the country's burgeoning middle and upper classes belie the government's efforts to present an aura of stationary Vietnamese consumption patterns (see Nguyen-Marshall, Drummond, and Bélanger 2012). However, the policies have been persuasive to the non-state tourism actors who are in part mediated through them.

The second portion of this chapter follows the first. If the đổi mới policies have restructured the national economy to make people who weren't previously well off rich (or richer), but that they have also presented the Vietnamese culture of consumption as unsusceptible to change, how do employees in the tourism industry arrange Vietnamese national identities given that some of its own residents now have the same spending power and leisure opportunities as foreigners? The answer lies in the utilization of stereotypes of Vietnam's burgeoning middle-upper and upper-classes as infringers on the tourism landscape. Vietnamese tourists are national citizens and thus have the ability to access Vietnamese culture as any insider would. However, Vietnamese middle and upper-class tourists are seen as adversely tampering with Vietnamese culture because they are interested in consuming Vietnam like an outsider. Moreover, Vietnamese tourists lack an interest in re-creating the typical performances that Western tourists display in Vietnam. Being an insider and outsider places Vietnamese domestic tourists in a doubly isolating position: they are seen as meddling with the outside and the inside and thus disrupt the fixity of this oppositional dialectic that is imparted by the actors in the tourism industry. However, this trick also places Vietnamese tourists in a doubly privileged position: Vietnamese people, whether tourists or not, are defaulted to a cultural insider position. Propagating stereotypes of Vietnamese tourists enacted by Ho Chi Minh City's tour guides do something to resolve the contradictions that Vietnamese tourists have placed on the country's tourism industry.

A brief conclusion will focus on the implications of these changing identities on category generation and upkeep. Interviews with a swath of tourism industry actors find that the largely abstract understandings of the national đổi mới policies and the grounded realities of the changing tourist sociodemographics in Ho Chi Minh City muddy the distinction between "traditional" culture and "progressive" economies. Categories of insiders and outsiders in the Vietnamese tourism industry emerge out of practices and discourses among actors such as the ones in the tourism industry rather than existing as stable preconditions in which identities can be neatly placed.

## VIETNAM'S "LATECOMER STATUS" AND THE RISE OF THE TOURISM INDUSTRY

Woodside (1999), in a comparative analysis of Vietnam and China after reform, argues that Vietnam's political elite have chosen to harness the country's economic achievements through đổi mới by calling itself a "latecomer state." It is a phrase generally used by the Vietnamese government to describe its integration into the global economy. The phrase attaches meanings of fast, efficient progress to Vietnam's đổi mới policy package. Woodside posits that this latecomer status and correlative definition of quick "catch-up" economic time-keeping is a "sort of national instrument of consciousness (that) is prominent in Vietnamese thought" (1999: 35). This comment suggests that the đổi mới policy package's reforms have done something for the collective economic ideology of Vietnam as well as lining individual pocketbooks and wallets. Being a latecomer state to the global economy underscores that Vietnam has been welcomed as an economic partner and as an investment opportunity despite its prior insular economic ideologies in the 1970s and 1980s.

The Vietnamese government spins the đổi mới policy package's methodical nature yet high-speed, progressive route into the global ranks as an effective, socialist-based, and inimitable set of policies in anything but a Vietnamese context. DiGregorio, Rambo, and Yanagisawa translate a prominent billboard in Hanoi that explained đổi mới to passersby this way: "Industrialization and modernization should not be considered goals in themselves, but rather as the means of creating 'rich people, strong country, fair and civilized society'" (2003: 171). This example represents a unique discourse of a national economic policy directive that attempts to present two paradoxical foci: speedy integration into the global economy while carefully overseeing policy formulation and implementation. In theory these avenues are of concern to the Vietnamese government in order to maintain a distinct Vietnamese identity amidst the windfall of openness and global integration that they are experiencing. The imaginings of a safeguarding of the inside against foreign investment outsiders solidify under these lines of thinking.

The Vietnamese government has evidently convinced many tourism operators to fall in line with its economic and cultural ideological make-up. A director of marketing named Pete at a large international tourism company in Ho Chi Minh City offhandedly remarked to me during an interview, "Vietnam is doing things well. Doing the transition well, I mean. There is still the Communist Party, so they aren't asking for much or rushing into much either." The implication to this comment is that outsiders are the ones going about the "doing" in Vietnam, in this case investing, and this allows the Vietnamese economy to flourish relatively quickly in the international economy. This phenomenon occurs while the Vietnamese government steps back and monitors these developments. In effect the state allows change to happen through the đổi mới policies that accept foreign investment but does not proactively pursue financial opportunities.

In the minds of members of the state, as the đổi mới initiatives have matured the overriding rhetoric of acceptance of foreign investment has begun to have adverse consequences for the country's cultural identity. This point has been made at length in chapter 3 but it bears a brief re-hashing here: for Vietnam's national government the monitoring of culture as a by-product of fiscal openness has become imperative to the country's development. The Vietnamese government uses a discourse of national culture (that is implemented in national policies) to point to Vietnamese people as the country's cultural providers, with direction and oversight from the state.

Who then is best in line to preserve Vietnam's cultural traditions seems obvious, especially in light of some of the state's leadership worrying about cultural detritus coming in from the outside after economic openness. The preservation of Vietnamese national culture is an intensely personal endeavor: cultural preservation relates to self-strengthening in that the strengthening of the self fortifies Vietnamese national culture writ large. In other words, if a Vietnamese person embodies Vietnamese cultural ideals (however defined), the person will be acting to maintain the Vietnamese national cultural system. This is a national project without class prejudices. Thus it is up to all Vietnamese to function for their country as bastions and promoters of national culture. The state has long formulated its cultural preservation policies through a repeated pattern of negative outside cultural influence and đổi mới has been the most recent in a string of rhetorical devices used to protect the government's power over Vietnam's shifting cultural-economy. These cultural responsibilities are perhaps most clearly placed among those working in Vietnam's tourism industry because they must respond to foreigners and their needs, they compete for business within the country and also with tourism players in other Southeast Asian countries, and they are in charge of interpreting, performing, and sharing culture with domestic and foreign guests every day.

This emphasis on cultural preservation plays an important role in the shaping of the Vietnamese political economy at both the abstract, policy-formulation levels, and at the scale of daily life in Vietnam. The Vietnamese government has been crafty in presenting outside investment and corresponding ideologies of "free markets" and "freedom" as carefully regulated in a cultural context once it enters the Vietnamese market. Thus, the force and tone of their anxiety regarding outside cultural influence has changed from the inception of the đổi mới policies not least of all because they have a broad swath of eager international investors and consumers waiting to sink their teeth into Vietnam's markets.

As mentioned in earlier chapters, in Vietnam culture and national identity don't necessarily need to be fully defined and explained as long as the state can frame outside cultural influences strategizing to upset it. For the Vietnam government "foreignness" is as much as they give in their argument to preserve Vietnamese culture, but it may be all that they need: the term's ambiguity serves as an umbrella to encompass many different strains of attack. While Vietnam's leadership is certainly not an exception among other state governments in building an ambiguous and useful culture, the state has cast the fluidity of its economy against a stable national culture in ways that promote an unequivocal dialectical separation of the two ideas. And the dialectic of an outside foreign culture impeding against a strong inside Vietnamese culture harks back to the chapter's main point: Vietnam's đổi mới policies have the effect of presenting Vietnamese consumerist culture as eternal and static, with forces acting against it. The state believes its culture is to be preserved and maintained and thus kept away from being prone to external exposure.

Moreover, the Vietnamese government perhaps considers their intended audiences more than the contents of the message itself when protecting Vietnam from outside influence. Consider this quote by Kerkvliet:

> Officials (in Vietnam) repeatedly emphasize, especially to foreigners, that people in Vietnam have considerable freedom to say and do what they like. They also argue that the state has a right and a duty to guard the nation against hostile domestic and international forces that hide behind a pretense of "human rights" and "democracy" to threaten peace and order and the country's hard-won independence and its social and economic improvements since the end of colonial rule and war. (Kerkvliet 2003: 39)

Though Kerkvliet does not mention culture specifically in his analysis, the oppositions of outside and inside are apparent in official descriptions of the presentation of Vietnamese freedom against "international forces," and that the construction and maintenance of the Vietnamese inside has been a torturous struggle against foreign interlocutors who are not able to understand the ways in which Vietnamese residents are able to exert their freedoms.

What the outside seems to be doing to Vietnam is pushing a rampant culture of consumption. Consumption and culture are uniquely intertwined in Vietnam and serve as both the backbone for solidifying Vietnam's traditions and for barricading certain practices, businesses, and ideologies from the outside that could contaminate the Vietnamese cultural body. The family (*gia đình*) is the most often cited representation of Vietnamese culture by respondents, a group that embodies the insider-outsider and culture-economy dialectics. Historically understood in many arenas as a group whose whole is greater than the sum of its parts, the idea of family is the most important influence on Vietnamese identity, culturally speaking or otherwise (Jamieson 1995). Thus, other scholars write that the identification of what Vietnamese culture "isn't" is commonly associated with individualism, unchecked consumption habits, and urbanity while what Vietnamese culture "is" is the countryside, re-productions of traditions, and an emphasis on family. Drummond posits that:

> The gap between urban and rural lifestyles has seemed to be widening almost daily, with urbanites leading progressively more luxurious and modern lifestyles compared with the constrained access to facilities which is only slowly improving the rural areas. Yet, it is a recurrent cultural theme in Vietnam, and one which is often reiterated in popular culture, that urban almost always equals bad, and rural equals good. Urban society is cold, modern, and stressful; rural society is warm, traditional and timeless, and peaceful. This characterization intersects with the perception of urban life as spiritually or morally bankrupt, as lacking a spiritual or ideological center that would hold urban society together as a civilized entity. (2003: 163)

If this is so then it follows that Vietnamese culture is concentrated in rural areas (the inside) and lacking in urban spaces (the outside) and that the inside should not be given up to outside interlopers (see Harms 2011).

## THE HO CHI MINH CITY TOURISM INDUSTRY AND THE RESOLUTION OF INSIDE AND OUTSIDE CONTRADICTIONS

Discourses that float the ideologies of insider and outsider status gain purchase in stereotypical languages and the case of the Ho Chi Minh City tourism industry is no exception. The Vietnamese tourist—armed with capital and vastly different knowledges, histories, and personal geographies of Vietnam than foreign tourists—form a decidedly strange character amidst the distinctions carved between consumptive and productive bodies in the city's tourism industry since the maturation of đổi mới. The categories of inside and outside are on display in discussions of tourists in the city and, like the state's rhetoric with respect to tourists and residents, achieve some sort of solidity through the employment of the inside-outside dialectic. However, recent changes to both the material landscapes and to perceptions of the tourist represent a significant blip in this dialectical construction. There is an interlocutor that influences the economic and the cultural dimensions of the country and of the inside and outside category: the Vietnamese domestic tourist. This shift is "out of place" in Vietnam in the ontological framework of category generation and in the material practices that coalesce around these categories. I offer an example of changes among classes as they interrupt the formed dialectic of inside and outside. I then illustrate how the tourism industry applies stereotypes to Vietnamese tourists—that they are difficult to work with, demanding of their guides, and spend all of their money—in order to restabilize the dialectic of the inside and outside.

*Vietnamese domestic tourists: personifying the inside and the outside?*

Vietnamese tourists are a relatively new phenomenon in the collective mindset of the Ho Chi Minh City tourism industry. Before đổi mới was enacted Vietnam's state-run tourism companies had a unique task: they issued travel permits to Vietnamese residents if they wanted to visit another area of Vietnam (Luong 2009). This imposing rule—in place for over twenty years—assisted in defining the boundaries of Vietnamese insider and foreign outsider in stark terms. Moreover, the travel permit rule was only applied to civilians and was waived for Vietnamese government officials and war heroes and their families. Foreign tourists, though regulated through a lengthy visa process, in many senses could conceive of Vietnam as "travelable" in ways that the Vietnamese could not. Foreigners need only pay a visa fee and fill out an application to be welcomed to most parts of the country. For a majority of Vietnamese nationals the roadblocks to travel were more diverse than a simple monetary payment and written application process. The obvious power and political authority over human movements that the state tourism operators had under these conditions notwithstanding, this sort of "offering" isn't typical of most tourism operators throughout the world. State-run companies do not offer permits to Vietnamese residents anymore but the historical context of having to ask the state for permission to travel—let alone to travel for leisure and consumption purposes—still forms part of the context behind travel and tourism in Vietnam and its historical significance has contributed to the idea of the Vietnamese citizen as a grounded, immobile, and culturally significant being.

Examples from field research supplement the point that in the Ho Chi Minh City tourism market Vietnamese residents aren't considered progressive tourists that desire to consume Vietnamese culture. A tourism operator I spoke with refuses to handle any Vietnamese tourist business and only serves Western markets. In Tài's words, "Vietnamese tourists are a growing segment but in Vietnam they are not categorized yet. The segment creates a lot of headaches and is difficult to deal with correctly." Another respondent, an independent tour guide named Bác, echoed Tài's statements: "They (the Vietnamese) drink all the time. Even on the bus! They drink all day long. It is so hard to keep the drunks on the bus and in order. They have to go to the bathroom, want more (to drink). We never make it to the destination and when we do they don't even look at it . . . they sit and drink together." The tension between Vietnamese tourists infringing on the tourism landscape—constructed and driven by outsiders—and their disruptive, as-yet-unrecognizable form provides a window into the ways in which the contemporary Vietnamese tourist has disrupted the dialectical opposition between insider and outsider. Tài presents the Vietnamese tourist as uncategorizable. How can the Vietnamese tourist be categorized as a tourist consumer when s/he is already categorically stabilized as a cultural provider? Cultural forms are heterogeneous and constantly in flux but according to the Vietnamese state and many Ho Chi Minh City tourism operators the stability of the relationship between insider and outsider is the crux of the Vietnamese tourism industry, especially in a place like Ho Chi Minh City where adverse cultures can easily enter on the backs of foreign capital. Tài has imbued meaning into the category of Vietnamese tourist by rendering it a non-category, one not allowed or desired to be placed within the stable distinctive category of tourist outsider.

In Bác's case, the Vietnamese tourist is a pariah in his or her own country. Drunkenness and alcohol consumption are not behaviors that Bác associates with the consumption of the cultural landscape and it is apparent in his incredulity that this is deviant tourist behavior. In our discussion that morning Bác's tone was one of discomfort but not of a sinister nature. Rather it was a perspective of astonishment, as if his conceptions of who tourists are, how they are served, and what their practices include are disrupted every time he takes domestic tourists on a trip. Despite my repeated attempts to bring the interview back to the subject of Vietnamese tourists, we did not discuss much about domestic tourists after his initial explanation to me. His answer was repeated verbatim, "they drink so much!" and it seemed that it was difficult for him to fill out the answer much further. This limited response suggests that he is not yet ready to cohere a perspective on local tourists but that their performances upset the categories of tourism and consumption that are sustained through his work. Tài and Bác's narratives reflect the changing dynamics of the Vietnamese tourism industry. Their positions as workers in the construction, repair, and presentation of the inside-outside dialectic in the tourism industry in part facilitate definitions of who Vietnamese tourists are and how their actions are understood. As Vietnamese are becoming more upwardly mobile and travel more frequently tourism actors like Tài and Bác are employing stereotypes to reinforce the scaffolding that constructs who inhabits the inside and outside categories of the Vietnamese tourist landscape.

*Utilizing stereotypes in the Ho Chi Minh City tourism industry to reconnect broken categories*

The stereotype of the Vietnamese tourist as "difficult to deal with" is a trope that many tourism operators in Ho Chi Minh City utilize to resolve the tensions that arise when a Vietnamese citizen develops the financial capital, social status, and free time to become a tourist-consumer of Vietnamese culture. John, the director of another long-running tourism company in the city, eschews setting up contracts for tours with Vietnamese residents. For him, there is "no incentive to have Vietnamese (on a tour), they are too demanding." Although our interview did not converge toward further discussion of what Vietnamese tourists are demanding of (and of whom), one can surmise that the Vietnamese tourists John is speaking of are directing their demands toward the local tourism industry's primary cultural suppliers, the tour guide (Salazar 2010). Vietnamese tour guides are quintessential cultural producers because they are the "face" of Vietnam for tourists. They are the physical representations of Vietnam. In fact, they are more than a representation of Vietnam: they embody the country in their mannerisms, their ability to "bridge cultures" between Vietnam and the foreign tourist, and siphon knowledge through themselves to the tourist. The clash between the tour guide who is the embodiment of Vietnamese culture and the "difficult" Vietnamese tourist presupposes John's refusal to "deal" with them.

Thus, a common stereotype employed by Ho Chi Minh City tourism actors is that Vietnamese tourists are more difficult on their guides than Western tourists are. Guides in Ho Chi Minh City are defensive when they relay their interactions with Vietnamese tourists to me. A tourism company owner named Hưng explained one story this way. One of his tour guides had taken a small tour out from Ho Chi Minh City to the Mekong Delta. It was a Sunday in late summer, considered the low season in Vietnamese tourism. This coincides with the time period when Vietnamese—whose children are on summer holiday and who have vacation time available—often take their holidays. Sundays are also the most common rest day in Ho Chi Minh City. It is a day when tour guides prefer not to work because there are often get-togethers, parties, family events, and relaxing that provide a chance to break from work. The obvious problems emerge:

> Hưng: We had a situation a few years ago where we couldn't get guides to work on Sundays unless they were doing a tour with Westerners. Guides don't like to work with other Vietnamese anyway . . .

Me: I was under the impression that the guides have some sort of a contractual agreement with you.

Hưng: Not really. All of our contracted guides were out that day because they have the Australians and other foreigners (to serve) first. The Vietnamese tourists were left over without anyone to take them to the (Mekong) Delta.

Me: Was it because the guides didn't want to work or because they didn't want to work with Vietnamese?

Hưng: Guides sometimes say no to work when it involves other Vietnamese.

Me: Why?

Hưng: Vietnamese tourists don't normally like the guides. (They) don't think they are necessary. Everyone knows everything already, in their minds. So the guides don't get tips, they have to go buy food, wine, and run around for them. Most guides would rather stay home on Sunday anyway.

It is arguable that the Vietnamese tour guide is the embodiment of traditional Vietnamese culture and economic success. At once h/she is well-dressed, well spoken and versed in the English language, business-like in his approach to consumers, diligent in his/her work ethic, and practiced in relating to persons of other cultures and perspectives. On the other hand, it is the work of the Vietnamese tour guide to offer Vietnamese culture in traditional ways to the tourist, whether by taking the group to a local market, to watch coconut candy made or farmers tending to their paddy fields, to listen to traditional Vietnamese music or a storyteller remark on the importance of family life, and so on. The Vietnamese tour guide harnesses the twin policies of economic fluidity and cultural fixity in his/her practices and in a sense "performs" the đổi mới policy package to tourists. This dialectical opposition collapses when the tour guide presenter must face Vietnamese citizens who themselves blur these distinctions. In these situations Vietnamese tour guides cannot call upon either their knowledge of a foreign language (as an outsider) or their gift of storytelling when describing Vietnam's past (as an insider). Hưng's way of resolving the destruction of this neat opposition is that the guides under his direction are not treated well by their fellow Vietnamese and therefore are neglected as clients for his company.

Luong argues that wealth differences in Ho Chi Minh City are historically greater than in Vietnam's capital, Hanoi. He goes on to say that there is "hidden wealth" in Ho Chi Minh City (2003: 85, and see Gainsborough [2010], Luong [2009]). Although he does not go into detail about this comment, it leads one to question who is doing the hiding and who is conscious of southern Vietnam's supposed wealth. More than likely we can posit that Vietnamese residents living and working in Ho Chi Minh City would have the greatest knowledge about these financial disparities, the depth and breadth of affluence in their city, and the means by which to best access wealth. Moreover, Luong's comment suggests that there are wealth differences in Hanoi as well as in Ho Chi Minh City, but without the extremes that exist in Ho Chi Minh City. The interviews I have conducted with tourism operators narrate stories (that have become formalized into stereotypes) of Vietnamese tourists spending copious amounts of money on tourism excursions while touring in the city. These narratives inform Luong's argument that Ho Chi Minh City residents have greater discretionary income than their compatriots in the north, but they take his position further: Ho Chi Minh City's residents spend this excess capital illegitimately. In contrast Western tourists are explained as conscious and refined (if also generous) in their purchasing choices. These stereotypes provide a collective lens into the changing nature of the insider-outsider dialectic and reinforce the need for the members of the city's tourism industry to continually structure their worlds around this stable dialectic.

For example, it was the end of May and the high season for international tourism to Ho Chi Minh City was coming to an end. The dreaded "low season" was approaching. With it was to come more sporadic and shorter-term employment for contracted guides (for example, half-day trips to the Cu Chi Tunnels were more prevalent than week-long ventures around the south). Because money was going to be tight for tour guides like Hiệp and his family throughout the summer he expected to move into his second mode of employment, which was teaching English at a local high school in the evenings. He was clearly displeased as he discussed these circumstances with me. I asked him how many tours he could reasonably expect to lead during the summer. This question spurred him on to a sour lament:

> Hiệp: Who can be sure? Some people (tour guides) never get a tour throughout the summer. The Vietnamese travel domestically. You know something about them? The Vietnamese spend all of their money when they go on holiday. Incredible! They save their money for a long time and then they spend it on their holiday. Every bit of it!
> Me: Why is that?
> Hiệp: They have a bad way of keeping their money. Instead of buying a better motorbike or spending money on education they spend it at the beach, drinking. No one cares.
> Me: Do they spend money on the trips?
> Hiệp: (hesitating) Not really because they know where to get things more cheaply. There is not much that they buy on the trip.
> Me: So they have more money to pay you better tips then?
> Hiệp: (with laughter) Of course not!
> Me: Does this problem happen throughout the country? (suggesting outside of Ho Chi Minh City as well)
> Hiệp: Of course! (personal communication)

I have repeatedly come across this complaint from tour guides, executives, desk employees, and even college students majoring in tourism. Why would such a notion about Vietnamese tourists be so pervasive and why? There are certainly emotive considerations to take into account on the part of the tourism industry collective. Jealousy, desire, and pettiness spring to mind. However, emotions have a tendency to vary widely in their style and substance and in the interviews and participant observations there has been a repetitive, distanced uniformity during our discussions of Vietnamese tourists' lack of frugality. Increased and varied personal expenditures correlate to a country's financial growth, so this aspect can be (at least partially) dismissed in the analysis. This brings us to the cultural aspects of tourism and it is at this point that it can again be argued that complaints about overspending reflect the disturbance of the Vietnamese cultural project. Newly minted Vietnamese tourists are not purchasing the cultural trinkets at stands littered throughout their prescribed paths at inflated prices, they are not lauding Vietnamese cultural sites, and they are not tipping their guides, drivers, or tour operator support staff in "appropriate" sums as "real" tourists. In sum, they are not replaying the culturally specific performances that their non-Vietnamese tourist counterparts are. Purchases along tourism routes have special significance for the tour guide: he/she usually gets a portion of the sellers' take on an informal commission basis. And there is a satisfaction from all parties (buyers, sellers, and guides) that a material culture purchase will allow tourists to keep their cultural experience long after their trip is over through locally made foods or handicrafts like chopsticks, glassware, or artwork. Instead, Vietnamese tourists are following *some* of their non-Vietnamese tourist spending habits: they are buying alcohol, upgrading their meals, staying in higher-end hotels, traveling to more destinations, and securing more days per year for travel. Certain tourism traits fall into the culturally unaware yet financially sound "outsider" category (desiring modern, high-end hotels rather than those with "history" or heritage, for instance) while others continue to inform the Vietnamese insider perspective (like the refusal to tip individuals for their work). Thus the need for stereotypical language when invoking the Vietnamese tourist; the borders between insider and outsider have been tarnished through the practices of this new, strange body of tourist.

## CONCLUSION

A new segment of tourist has entered Vietnam's tourism industry ill-equipped with the understandings and perceptions that foreign tourists carry. Foreign tourists and their Vietnamese local tourism support have been successful in constructing distinctive boundaries around their identities: the Vietnamese are the knowledgeable, culturally sound insider and the foreigner (usually Western) is the rich and culturally depraved outsider. These oppositional categories have done the work of propelling the tourism industry forward since the advent of đổi mới, and with historical roots traced back even further. The đổi mới policies and their authors have been complicit in this dialectical construction by grounding it in an ideology of the state, which is still the biggest provider of tours in Ho Chi Minh City and Vietnam.

In scaling out to form a more theoretically informed conclusion there seem to be two ways to go about assessing the consequences for this insider-outsider binary: the oppositional boundaries drawn around insider and outsider are not limits but regulated, permeable passageways or conversely, that the boundaries themselves aren't as much at stake as what flows through them or accumulates in them. The regulations of these boundaries have been institutionalized by the Vietnamese state that regards Vietnamese culture as a definitive, coherent body to be maintained throughout the dramatic financial transformations occurring in the country. Part of the way the state has been successful in this endeavor is by connecting it to the country's leading segment of the cultural economy, the tourist industry and its workers. But this is no mere regurgitation of the state's policies. Rather, it is the Ho Chi Minh City tourism actors' attempt to make sense of and perpetuate the categories they themselves have built into their professional lives. The đổi mới policies inform but do not produce them. Their daily lives do.

All this said there are doubtless incredible changes occurring within this dialectic. The seemingly secure categories of insider and outsider are in truth the opposite; in flux, made and remade, collapsed, redefined, and bleeding into each other in myriad ways. The categories are constructed from dramatically emergent properties that are the scaffolding for the (re)formulation of Vietnamese and tourist identities. As the scaffolding is collapsing, so the categories follow. Vietnamese tourism actors—who have an important hand in their creation and upkeep—are working hard through their everyday professional lives to understand these changes with an eye toward an imagined coherency. In this way the categories acquire a strange dimension, imagined as stable yet pulled and tugged in innumerable directions. The categories of insider and outsider, then, do include a hint of permanence despite their unstable underpinnings.

## NOTE

Parts of this chapter were previously published as Jamie Gillen, "A Battle worth Winning: The Service of Culture to the Communist Party of Vietnam in the Contemporary Era," *Political Geography* 30, no. 5 (2011).

# SEVEN

## Conclusion

This manuscript has centered on the entrepreneurial activities among non-state or private tourism actors in the context of the hybrid cultural-economy of Ho Chi Minh City. Ho Chi Minh City is a city where culture and economy are mutually constituted at all levels of social life, entangling policies and practices; insider/outsider and domestic/foreign dialectical oppositions; painful memories and hopeful futures; nascent and late capitalism; and national and expedient cultures. The roles actors play in urban entrepreneurialism have been highlighted and this approach shifts the perspective from state and urban governance to private actors who conceive of and utilize culture and economy's entanglement in their pursuit of prosperity. In turn, the cultural-economy approach to Ho Chi Minh City's urban life upsets traditional notions of the urban economy from both a cultural standpoint and from the actors involved in the urban economy's formation. Additionally, following the hybrid urban cultural-economy demonstrates some of the weaknesses of the traditional considerations of entrepreneurial cities because the model holds culture on a separate and diminished plane from the capitalist economy. Similarly, in typical models of entrepreneurial cities the political-economic practices of urban governments usually receive analytic precedence over non-state "private" firms, something that is rectified through these chapters. Indeed it has been a prevailing tendency to privilege the state in many studies of the political economy of Vietnam during the đổi mới period and beyond (see Malesky and London 2014, Tai and Sidel 2012, Beeson and Hung 2012).

The manuscript's conclusion includes two parts. The first section visits two empirical studies of non-state actors in other parts of urban Southeast Asia in order to debunk the possible Vietnamese exceptionalism that may be apparent in my critique of entrepreneurial cities. Throughout the

Southeast Asian region non-state actors contest "national" readings of culture, differentiate themselves from the government and from competitors in their pursuit of success, and work together with a variety of actors and firms as they go about commodifying places for tourists. I then wrap up by comparing this manuscript's conceptualization of neoliberalism with other recent work done on the relationship between Vietnam and its supposed "neoliberal" governance (e.g., Schwenkel and Leshkowich 2012).

*Is Ho Chi Minh City's urban cultural-economy unique? Evidence from other transitional urban economies in Southeast Asia*

Vietnamese studies scholars often insist that the Vietnamese political economy does not resemble those of its Southeast Asian neighbors (to say nothing of the Western world) because it has transformed so remarkably from a command to a market economy. For example, Beresford begins a chapter in an edited volume on Southeast Asia this way: "Vietnam is unique among the countries covered in this book in that it is in the process of transition from central planning to a market economy" (Beresford 2006: 197). Others emphasize Vietnam's uniqueness in Southeast Asia if not in Asia as a whole. China—the world's biggest "market socialist" country—is frequently considered Vietnam's most appropriate national comparative study because of its ability to manage centralized control over the market economy. For example, Beeson and Hung argue, "In many ways . . . the concentration of state control in Vietnam mirrors similar developments in China" (2012: 551 and see Yeo and Painter 2011, McGee 2009). Similarly, Zhang's recent article on "postsocialist assemblages" aligns China and Vietnam together in terms of their similar paths toward a market economy and their marginal treatment in the majority of research conducted on postsocialist states (Zhang 2012).

At the same time, other countries in Southeast Asia are discounted as "similar" to one another or unable to manage their economic and political transitions in the same way as Vietnam. For example, in many circles it is argued that Malaysia is already "more developed" than Vietnam by virtue of its expansive high-tech corridor surrounding Kuala Lumpur as well as its ability to attract a range of different visitors by offering a rich mix of tourism, leisure, and investment options (Ormond 2013). The Philippines, Indonesia, and Thailand have established democratic but politically fractious states, making them arguably less safe and stable for investment and tourism opportunities than Vietnam (Hall and Page 2011, Keese 2011, Sonmez 1998). Laos, Cambodia, and East Timor are mired in poverty, agrarianism, and challenging infrastructure problems. Singapore is in a distinct category itself (as a venerable "Asian Tiger") because of its high gross domestic product, quality of life, political stability, and status as a transportation and tourist hub in the region (Chua 2011,

Chang and Yeoh 1999, though see Gainsborough 2009). Finally there is Myanmar, a country that is currently "opening up" to foreign investment and tourism but that has been politically authoritarian and economically isolated for a long time. If we are to take these arguments seriously, from a Southeast Asian perspective Vietnam is literally in a category by itself.

Digging deeper into the literature on Southeast Asia, however, one finds that many of the region's countries are experiencing dramatic shifts in their economies and much like the Vietnamese state other governments are maneuvering to continue their dominance over the direction of their markets. Additionally, non-state actors continue to create new opportunities on the backs of informal networks that are injected with cultural-economic inputs. Lest this work align itself with Vietnamese exceptionalism in the region, two examples from Siem Reap, Cambodia, and Kuala Lumpur, Malaysia, demonstrate that Ho Chi Minh City's cultural-economy shares many characteristics with its Southeast Asian neighbors. These examples illustrate two things: the precedence of "culture" in national politics throughout Southeast Asia and the tension between national and urban-inflected cultural expediencies in the region.

Tim Winter's work in Siem Reap, Cambodia, draws on the remarkable increases in international and regional Asian tourists to the city to illustrate the differences between governmental policies aimed at structuring the Siem Reap cultural-economy to cater to wealthy, ostensibly foreign tourists and the entrepreneurial "flows" of the private sector that seek to create a niche for less-affluent Asian tourists (Winter 2008, 2007). While not using Yúdice's cultural expedient position explicitly, Winter's work is much like the arguments in this monograph in that he argues that the Cambodian government attempts to control infrastructure development, financial inflows, and the types of firms operating in Cambodia's premier tourist destination, Angkor Wat (outside Siem Reap) through discourses of culture. As an example, Winter points to the Authority for the Protection and Safeguarding of the Angkor Region (APSARA), an appendage of the Cambodian government-run body charged with developing the Angkor area. In December 2000, APSARA gathered members of the Cambodian government, international consultants, and state representatives from the Middle East, Europe, and Asia for a conference to explain the "cultural tourism" model of economic growth in Angkor. During the meeting the director of APSARA's tourism department declared:

> tourism in Cambodia must first and foremost be *cultural* tourism. . . .
> The policy of cultural tourism that Cambodia intends to implement must have specific goals in order to prevent it from turning into commercial tourism . . . [we must] . . . promote quality cultural tourism, and avoid mass tourism by raising the level of accommodation and the quality of services offered (cited in Winter 2007: 35).

This call equates cultural tourism (not commercial tourism) with the construction of a tourist zone where tourists can spend their money on high-end retail, Cambodian heritage artifacts, and populate international hotel chains like Accor and Four Seasons (Winter 2007: 36).

The invitation list for the APSARA conference was small and targeted to players staked in the luxury tourism niche. Cultural tourism is distinguished from commercial tourism in order to recruit only international companies, thereby validating the Cambodian government's plans to create a special tourist "zone" in Siem Reap that appeals to calls by environmental and heritage organizations like United Nations Educational, Scientific and Cultural Organization (UNESCO) to raise their standards and minimum requirements for tourism company performance in the area. Cultural tourism also hints at a more authentic version of tourism than conventional commercial tourism, thereby creating an official sphere for the Cambodian government to categorize those companies it deems "cultural" (transnational, luxury) and those it deems more "commercial" (mid- and low-range). Cultural tourism provides an avenue for the Cambodian government to weave together Angkor and its tourist "zones" into a high-end heritage destination unique to Southeast Asia. Winter continues his arguments by showing that the "cultural tourism framework being offered during this period was principally conceived around, and driven by, the pragmatics of providing high quality services" (Winter 2007: 35). Winter's research divulges that high-quality services translate into high-cost services, a connection introduced by Cambodian officials whose vision of the rich economic potential in Angkor has been conditioned by UNESCO's and lending organizations' insistence that they address the swelling tourism population through strict, enforced regulations concerning which (transnational) companies can operate in the area.

Winter goes on to describe the "flows" that challenge the government's intended tourism structure in Siem Reap. Flows for Winter include the conglomeration of people, firms, technologies, knowledges, and imageries that congeal (often transnationally) to produce localized action (Urry 2003: 60, cited in Winter 2007: 29). He writes that non-state Cambodian, Chinese, Korean, Malaysian, and other Asian entrepreneurs create interconnected networks that usurp Cambodia's national policies aimed at erecting an exclusive, well-off, Western tourism community. Recognizing the tremendous tourism potential in the Asian market yet without the official means or established geographical area to extend services to Asian consumers, these entrepreneurs have opened businesses outside of the government-decreed "tourist zone," filled them with Korean, Chinese, and Japanese language-speaking employees, and have used "informal partners" to manage (or sidestep) the regulations the government has put into place (Winter 2007: 39). Siem Reap landowners have often decided to sell their property to these Asian transnational groups rather than the Cambodian government and its multinational partners because these informal networks have streamlined the process from discovery to acquisition to a much greater extent than the Cambodian government has (*ibid.*). These flows allow Asian entrepreneurs to innovate and construct market niches around a specific category of consumer outside of the framework of an appropriate, state-defined cultural tourism model. Winter does not directly address the ways in which these networks form nor the steps they take to navigate through the bureaucratic levels, but the result is clear: "the gap which has formed between the rigid (institutions) of policy and the more fluid, organic flows of an entrepreneurial investment culture has been pivotal in shaping the ways in which capital has spatially embedded itself across the Siem Reap urban landscape" (*ibid.*).

The Cambodia case is similar to Vietnam's in a number of ways. First, the Cambodian government's "culture-as-resource" mimics the Vietnamese state's contradictory yet intentional evocation of culture. APSARA's director seems unconcerned with explaining or being held responsible for the conceptual differences between "cultural" and "commercial" tourisms. These designations are codes: cultural tourism is high-quality, expensive, has distinct geographic boundaries, and commercial tourism is everything else. Secondly, networks that cater to Asian tourists entertain loose and fluid types of configurations without the official dressing of their state-run counterparts. No less valuable, these networks are highly entrepreneurial in character and execution (Winter 2007: 38). Crucially, they also include the formalities of national policy as these flow arrangements steer through bureaucratic channels in order to establish and maintain their own businesses. Winter eschews describing these networks as active "resistors" to the Cambodian government's policies because these groups seem to understand the inherent permeability of national tourism policies. To be sure, these policies seem more like chances for non-state coordination with the government because the policies set into motion opportunities for entrepreneurial activity on a variety of fronts and by an assortment of actors and organizations. Lastly, Winter does not take entrepreneurialism as a predetermined set of characteristics that are generated by urban governance practices and modeled on the activities of Asian tourism actor-networks. His respondents hint at the impermanence, the tenuousness, and the usefulness of their collaborations. Here the hybridized cultural-economy is critical to the production of the Siem Reap tourism industry. Relationships arise out of the economic knowledges of overseas Chinese, the local knowledges of Cambodians in Siem Reap, and the trust and accountability of contacts made through friends and family. These relationships have been developed as a result of increased visitors to Siem Reap but they are animated with the kinds of cultural-economic registers highlighted in earlier chapters.

In Malaysia, Lepawsky's dense analysis of the management of the Kuala Lumpur mega-project known as the Multimedia Super Corridor (MSC) illuminates the slippages between the subjectivities of transnational non-state actors and the "universal" urban design principles they represent through their contribution to the official Malaysian government planning document for the project entitled "Physical Design Guidelines for the Multimedia Super Corridor" (hereafter "Guidelines") (Lepawsky 2005). The MSC—a spectacular multi-billion dollar information technology and telecommunications area that covers 750 km$^2$ south of Kuala Lumpur—is part of a multifaceted package intended to drive Malaysia to fully developed status by 2020, peacefully unite all people in Malaysia into a single "Bangsa Malaysia" ("Malaysian race"), and keep Malaysians "in full possession of an economy that is competitive, dynamic, robust, and resilient. . . ." (cited in Lepawsky 2005: 705). The Guidelines are to encompass these principles through its notion of a "suburban, middle-class" design structure (*ibid.*). Reflecting the public sector-private enterprise coordination that occurs in many urban areas around the world, the components for the Guidelines were compiled by Malaysian government officials, Malaysian engineers and planners, and international consultants from firms in Australia, the United Kingdom, and the United States. On the surface, then, the Guidelines are a shining example of entrepreneurial urban governance: expensive and risky for the Kuala Lumpur and Malaysian governments, created by a variety of actors with divergent agendas, and aggressively marketed across a range of scales, from the urban to the regional to the international. The Guideline's directives suggest a complete Malaysian state vision of the future with their focus on a unified, ethnically homogeneous Malaysian state built on "strong moral and ethical values . . . caring, economically just and equitable, progressive and prosperous . . ." (Lepawsky 2005: 705).

Yet Lepawsky's interviews with two principal contributors to the Guidelines from a major USA urban planning firm show that the entrepreneurial program's design does not represent a universal Malaysian vision of the future. In the first place, these two planners take issue with the registers of moral values that pervade an urban entrepreneurial arrangement between the public and private sectors, or in Lepawsky's words "state and non-state interests" (2005: 710). Lepawsky's point isn't whether or not U.S. planners have moral values and the Malaysian government doesn't but that different understandings of business ethics between the two groups contrast sharply with the transcendental, universal discourse of the Malaysian economy portrayed in the Guidelines. One USA planner named Dan had this to say, "Things in Malaysia were really going strong up to the monetary crisis of 1997. They were working as hard as they could to 'showcase' Malaysia as the most progressive nation in Southeast Asia . . . (we) wrote the design guidelines (but) even at this, they took a long time to make the payment for this work . . ." (*ibid.*).

Another planner named Jim echoed Dan's problems with the MSC by lamenting, "we never were completely paid for our efforts" (*ibid.*).

In these statements the cultural-economic registers of moral sentiment and trust collide in a web of mismatched expectations. For Dan, payment for finished work on the Guidelines should be remitted in a timely fashion, calling into question the extent to which his particular version of "market rules" were understood and agreed upon with his Malaysian colleagues beforehand. Moreover, the problems with remittance between the Malaysian government and its U.S. consultants highlight the processual nature of the urban cultural-economy where grand claims on Malaysian universality, fixity, and impermeability are undercut by the mundane practices of actors, institutions, and places. For Lepawsky the purity of Malaysia's Guidelines—of, for, and created by Malaysians—is suspect when "it is difficult to pin the Guidelines to any single location or 'national context'" (2005: 709). This circulation is of greater importance than identifying general processes indicative to many urban areas throughout the world because "it cues one to the specificity of this collection of individuals and institutions and reminds one that these normative design principles do not represent a 'straight-forward' imposition of 'conventional' notions of urban space and subjectivity onto a new landscape" like the MSC (*ibid.*).

In Vietnam the national government presents a seamless national culture by refashioning history to include long-standing cultural pillars, describing its new policies as culturally sound, and projecting society's ills on foreign perpetrators. Similarly, Malaysian national identity is formed through the MSC, giving one the impression that the Guidelines are a universally Malaysian construction. Understanding the tenuous construction of these endeavors validates cultural-economic registers, where the mundane and the everyday complement the sweeping and the general in the narration of changes occurring in Southeast Asian countries like Cambodia, Malaysia, and Vietnam.

*Neoliberal governance and the Vietnamese state*

As noted in chapter 3, this manuscript takes a skeptical view that the Vietnamese government has adopted a neoliberal approach to overseeing the reform era. At its broadest I understand neoliberal governance to be the transfer of the management of the market from the state to private hands (Harvey 2005). Market rules and regulations are oriented more toward the profitability of the private sector than the equitable distribution of resources and services by the state. The state takes a backseat to the interests of private enterprise and correspondingly facilitates disparities in wealth, yet encourages an economically efficient and individualized form of self or personhood that grants rewards to those who apply "free" market logics to their own lives and careers. Following Gainsborough's work (2010, 2009, 2005), I have argued that the Vietnamese government has recalibrated its guidance of the Vietnamese economy rather than wholeheartedly surrendering it to privatization and the dictates of capital. In fact "guidance" may be the incorrect word to use in this instance because it suggests that the state is limited to establishing and enforcing market-related rules and is removed from profiting from the changes that have occurred when opening up the market during the đổi mới period. The "trick" the Vietnamese state has played (and one that flies in the face of typical understandings of neoliberal change) is that the state's version of market reform includes a substantial role for the government's market interests. While the dissolution of unprofitable state-owned enterprises has certainly occurred because of reform, these so-called neoliberal decisions have been matched with a substantial amount of differentiation among and expansion of state economic interests. Despite public announcements and decisions made to the contrary, the state continues to be both a regulator and a competitor in the marketplace.

This is not the end of the story, however. The state may maintain regulatory authority and be able to profit greatly from the reform period but those in the non-state category are also rewarded by the country's economic growth. Non-state actors are involved in ways both competitive and collaborative with members and logics of the state just as officials and rule-makers are interested in collaborating and competing with members of the private sector. The outwardly restrictive and rent-seeking advantages laid out by the state are in fact much weaker and more malleable than they may seem. Chapter 4 in particular sheds light on the ways in which interests among members of the state and non-state intersect along cultural-economic and entrepreneurial lines. The economy is driven as much by cultural forms of negotiation and change as they are by the so-called dominant forms of neoliberalism represented in the đổi mới policy package.

By way of a concluding comment, a recent special issue in *Positions: Asia Critique* on neoliberalism and Vietnam deserves attention and engagement. Edited by Schwenkel and Leshkowich, their prevailing concern is to ask "What is unique about "neoliberalism" in socialist Vietnam"? (2012: 381). Like my work, the authors outline "a marked ambivalence . . . toward use of the term neoliberalism, not only because (of) the extent to which Vietnam can even be considered neoliberal. . . . but also because of ongoing confusion about the term's meaning and implications" (*ibid.*). My study perhaps takes this point in a slightly different direction because I assume that neoliberalism is a "top-down" and managerial initiative that shifts authority from the state to market managers, private industry executives, and key gatekeepers in the revenue motives of for-profit institutions. Neoliberalism therefore doesn't make sense in Vietnam because this supposed shift—evident in the (false) assumptions of the reform era—masks the everyday cultural-economy playing out between non-state actors, individuals associated with the government, and private company leaders (among others). For the authors in this special issue, their point of departure rests primarily on the ways in which individuals unaffiliated with the state or big business embody neoliberal logics like individual accountability (Leshkowich 2012, Pashigian 2012), abide by "ethical" and anticorrupt market behaviors (MacLean 2012), and measure their successes according to the "morality" of the market rather than according to more-than-economic norms (Montoya 2012).

One similarity between my work and existing research on Vietnam's relationship to neoliberalism is that Vietnam resists easy categorization as a "market," "socialist," or even "market-socialist" economy. Schwenkel and Leshkowich opine that "new emergent forms of neoliberal capitalism in Vietnam defy in very particular ways oppositions between public and private, and socialist and capitalist, to reveal spheres of mutual constitution, juxtaposition, and coexistence" (2012: 384). Without going so far to say that the capitalism in Vietnam is neoliberal, this manuscript has traced the ways in which the Vietnamese economy unfolds in ways that make "easy" distinctions—most importantly between culture and economy—suspect and unproductive. Instead of relying on macro-economic definitions that largely arise out of late-capitalist and democratic societies I advocate a more nuanced and complicated understanding of the Vietnamese economy that moves beyond the socialist-capitalist spectrum. Vietnamese respondents in Leshkowich's work who explain that paying bribes and giving gifts "are creative Vietnamese ways of getting things done" (2012: 513) and that "in Vietnam there's a network of neighbors who oversee things very well . . . everyone knows what's going on in the families around them, so we don't need the kinds of inspections like they have abroad" (*ibid.*) are empirical kinds of shorthand for the goals in this monograph: there are crucial cultural and hybridized cultural-economic representations, performances, and activities that produce and embody the Vietnamese economy. Respondents in Leshkowich's research who share their versions of the Vietnamese economy, like the narratives from my respondents, bear scarce resemblance to conventional understandings of the market reform period. My overriding goal has been to offer some adjustments to the market reform period using examples from both the state (top-down) and the non-state (bottom-up) using the tourism industry, an industry that itself is tasked with representing Vietnamese culture and also has an important role to play in driving the country's economy.

# Bibliography

Agergaard, J., and Vu Thi Thao. (2011). "Mobile, Flexible, and Adaptable: Female Migrants in Hanoi's Informal Sector." *Population, Space, and Place* 17: 407-420.

Allen, J. (2002). Symbolic Economies: The 'Culturalization' of Economic Knowledge. *Cultural Economy: Cultural Analysis and Commercial Life*. P. du Gay, and M. Pryke, eds. London, Sage: 39-58.

Alneng, V. (2002). "What the Fuck Is a Vietnam? Touristic Phantasms and the Popcolonialization of (the) Vietnam (War)." *Critique of Anthropology* 22(4): 461-489.

Amin, A., and N. Thrift. (2007). "Cultural-Economy and Cities." *Progress in Human Geography* 31(2): 143-161.

Amin, A., and N. Thrift, eds. (2004). *Blackwell Cultural Economy Reader*. Oxford, Blackwell.

Baird, I. G., and P. Le Billon. (2012). "Landscapes of Political Memories: War Legacies and Land Negotiations in Laos." *Political Geography* 31: 290-300.

Barnes, T. (2006). Between Deduction and Dialectics: David Harvey on Knowledge. *David Harvey: A Critical Reader*. N. Castree & D. Gregory, eds. London, Blackwell: 26-46.

Barnes, T. (2005). Culture: Economy. *Spaces of Geographical Thought: Deconstructing Human Geography's Binaries*. P. Cloke, and R. Johnston, eds. London, Sage: 61-80.

Barnes, T. (2003). Never Mind the Economy. Here's Culture. *The Handbook of Cultural Geography*. K. Anderson, M. Domosh, S. Pile, and N. Thrift, eds. London, Sage: 89-97.

Beeson, M., and H. P. Hung. (2012). "Developmentalism with Vietnamese Characteristics: The Persistence of State-Led Development in East Asia." *Journal of Contemporary Asia* 42(4): 539-559.

Beresford, M. (2008). "Doi Moi in Review: The Challenges of Building Market Socialism in Vietnam." *Journal of Contemporary Asia* 38(2): 221-243.

Beresford, M. (2006). Vietnam: The Transition from Central Planning. *The Political Economy of South-East Asia: Markets, Power and Contestation*. G. Rodan, K. Hewison, and R. Robison, eds. Oxford, Oxford University Press: 197-220.

Bezmez, D. (2008). "The Politics of Urban Waterfront Regeneration: The Case of HaliĀç (the Golden Horn), Istanbul." *International Journal of Urban and Regional Research* 32(4): 815-840.

Biggs, D. (2012). *Quagmire: Nation-Building and Nature in the Mekong Delta*. Seattle, University of Washington Press.

Britton, S. (1991). "Tourism, Capital, and Place: Towards a Critical Geography of Tourism." *Environment and Planning D: Society and Space* 9: 451-478.

Butler, R., and W. Suntikul, eds. (2012). *Tourism and War*. London, Routledge.

Castree, N. (2004). "Economy and Culture Are Dead! Long Live Economy and Culture!" *Progress in Human Geography* 28(2): 204-226.

Chang, T. C., and B. Yeoh. (1999). "'New Asia-Singapore': Communicating Local Cultures Through Global Tourism." *Geoforum* 30(2): 101-115.

Chio, J. (2011). "The Appearance of the Rural in China's Tourism." *Provincial China* 3(1): 60-79.

Chua, B. H. (2011). Singapore as Model: Planning Innovations, Knowledge Experts. *Worlding Cities: Asian Experiments and the Art of Being Global*. A. Roy and A. Ong, eds. London, Blackwell: 29-54.

Cohen, E., and S. A. Cohen. (2012). "Current Sociological Theories and Issues in Tourism." *Annals of Tourism Research* 39(4): 2177-2202.

Dang N. M., and T. T. Pham. (2003). Representations of Doi Moi Society in Contemporary Vietnamese Cinema. *Consuming Urban Culture in Contemporary Vietnam.* L. Drummond and M. Thomas, eds. London, RoutledgeCurzon: 191-201.

DiGregorio, M., A. T. Rambo, and M. Yanagisawa. (2003). Clean, Green and Beautiful: Environment and Development Under the Renovation Economy. *Postwar Vietnam: Dynamics of a Transforming Society.* H. V. Luong, ed. Singapore, Institute of Southeast Asian Studies and Rowman and Littlefield Publishers, LLC: 171-200.

Drummond, L. B. W., and M. Thomas, eds. (2003). *Consuming Urban Culture in Contemporary Vietnam.* London, RoutledgeCurzon.

Drummond, L. (2003). Vietnamese Television Dramas and Images of Urban Life. *Consuming Urban Culture in Contemporary Vietnam.* L. Drummond and M. Thomas, eds. London, Routledge Curzon: 155-169.

Duncan, J. S. (1980). "The Superorganic in American Cultural Geography." *Annals of the Association of American Geographers* 76(2): 181-198.

Fforde, A. and S. De Vylder. (1996). *From Plan to Market: The Economic Transition in Vietnam.* Boulder, CO, Westview Press.

Freeman, D. B. (1996). "Doi Moi Policy and the Small-Enterprise Boom in Ho Chi Minh City, Vietnam." *Geographical Review* 86(2): 178-198.

Gainsborough, M. (2010). *Vietnam: Rethinking the State.* London, Zed Books.

Gainsborough, M. (2009). "The (Neglected) Statist Bias and the Developmental State: The Case of Singapore and Vietnam." *Third World Quarterly* 30(7): 1317-1328.

Gainsborough, M. (2005). "Between Exception and Rule." *Critical Asian Studies* 37(3): 363-390.

Gainsborough, M. (2003). *Changing Political Economy of Vietnam: The Case of Ho Chi Minh City.* London, Routledge Curzon.

Gibson, C. (2009). "Geographies of Tourism: Critical Research on Capitalism and Local Livelihoods." *Progress in Human Geography* 33(4): 527-534.

Gibson-Graham, J. K. (2006). *The End of Capitalism, As We Knew It: A Feminist Critique of Political Economy.* London, Blackwell.

Goscha, C. E. (1996). Annam and Vietnam in the New Indochine Space, 1887-1945. *Asian Forms of the Nation.* S. Tonneson and H. Antlov, eds. London, Curzon: 93-130.

Hall, C. M. (2008). "Pro-Poor Tourism: Do 'Tourism Exchanges Benefit Primarily the Countries of the South'?" *Current Issues in Tourism* 10(2 & 3): 111-118.

Hall, C. M., and S. Page, eds. (2011). *Tourism in South and Southeast Asia: Issues and Cases.* London, Routledge.

Hall, T., and P. Hubbard. (1996). "The Entrepreneurial City: New Urban Politics, New Urban Geographies?" *Progress in Human Geography* 20: 153-174.

Harms, E. (2013). "The Boss: Conspicuous Invisibility in Ho Chi Minh City." *City and Society* 25(2): 195-215.

Harms, E. (2012). "Neo-Geomancy and Real Estate Fever in Postreform Vietnam." *Positions: Asia Critique* 20(2): 405-434.

Harms, E. (2011). *Saigon's Edge: Space, Time, and Power on Ho Chi Minh City's Rural-Urban Margin.* Minneapolis, MN, University of Minnesota Press.

Harvey, D. (2006). "Neo-Liberalism as Creative Destruction." *Geografiska Annaler, Series B* 88(2): 145-158.

Harvey, D. (2005). *A Brief History of Neoliberalism.* Oxford, Oxford University Press.

Harvey, D. (1989). "From Managerialism to Entrepreneurialism: The Transformation in Urban Governance in Late Capitalism." *Geografiska Annaler* 71B: 3-17.

Hayton, B. (2010). *Vietnam: Rising Dragon.* New Haven, CT, Yale University Press.

He, S., and F. Wu. (2009). "China's Emerging Neoliberal Urbanism: Perspectives from Urban Redevelopment." *Antipode* 41(2): 282-304.

Hoang, K. K. (2011). "'She's Not a Low-Class Dirty Girl!': Sex Work in Ho Chi Minh City, Vietnam." *Journal of Contemporary Ethnography* 40(4): 367-396.

Hoang, K. K. (2015). *Dealing in Desire: Asian Ascendancy, Western Decline, and the Hidden Currencies of Global Sex Work*. Berkeley, University of California Press.

Hubbard, P. and T. Hall, eds. (1998). *The Entrepreneurial City: Geographies of Politics, Regime and Representation*. Chichester, John Wiley & Sons.

Jackson, P. (2004). "Local Consumption Cultures in a Globalizing World." *Transactions of the Institute of British Geographers* 29(2): 165-178.

Jamieson, N. J. (1995). *Understanding Vietnam*. Berkeley, University of California Press.

Judd, D. and R. L. Ready. (1986). Entrepreneurial Cities and the New Politics of Economic Development. *Reagan and the Cities*. G. E. Peterson and C. W. Lewis, eds. Washington, DC, Urban Institute Press: 209-247.

Keese, J. R. (2011). "The Geography of Volunteer Tourism: Place Matters." *Tourism Geographies* 13(2): 257-279.

Kennedy, L. B. and M. R. Williams. (2001). The Past Without Pain: the manufacture of nostalgia in Vietnam's Tourism Industry. *The Country of Memory: Remaking the Past in Late Socialist Vietnam*. H.-T. H. Tai, ed. Berkeley, University of California Press: 135-163.

Kerkvliet, B. J. (2005). *The Power of Everyday Politics: How Vietnamese Peasants Transformed National Policy*. Ithaca, NY, Cornell University Press.

Kerkvliet, B. J. (2003). Authorities and the People: An Analysis of State-Society Relations in Vietnam. *Postwar Vietnam: Dynamics of a Transforming Society*. H. V. Luong, ed. Lanham, MD, Rowman & Littlefield: 27-53.

Kerkvliet, B. J. (2001). "An Approach for Analysing State-Society Relations in Vietnam." *Sojourn* 16(2): 238-278.

Kerkvliet, B. J. T. and D. J. Porter, eds. (1995). *Vietnam's Rural Transformation*. Transitions: Asia and Asian America. Boulder, CO, Westview Press.

Kim, A. (2008). *Learning to be Capitalists: Entrepreneurs in Vietnam's Transition Economy*. Oxford, Oxford University Press.

Kim, S.-J., and J. Wainwright. (2010). "When Seed Fails: The Contested Nature of Neoliberalism in South Korea." *Geoforum* 41: 723-733.

Koh, D. (2001a). "Negotiating the Socialist State in Vietnam Through Local Administrators: The Case of Karaoke Shops." *Sojourn* 16(2): 279-305.

Koh, D. (2001b). "The Politics of a Divided Party and Parkinson's State in Vietnam." *Contemporary Southeast Asia* 23(3): 533-551.

Kwon, H. (2012). "Rethinking Traumas of War." *South East Asia Research* 20(2): 227-237.

Larsen, J., and J. Urry. (2011). "Gazing and Performing." *Environment and Planning D* 29: 1110-1125.

Le, K. (2014). "Cu Chi Tunnels: Vietnamese Transmigrant's Perspective." *Annals of Tourism Research* 46: 75-88.

Lê Khả Phiêu. (2005). "The Resolution of the Fifth Conference of the Party's Central Executive Board (session VIII) on Building and Developing an Advanced Vietnamese Culture, Which is Typical of the National Character," 8/16/2005. Communist Party of Vietnam.

Lee, S. -O., S-J Kim, and J. Wainwright (2010). "Mad Cow Militancy: Neoliberal Hegemony and Social Resistance in South Korea." *Political Geography* 29: 359-369.

Legg, S. (2005). "Contesting and Surviving Memory: Space, Nation, and Nostalgia in *Les Lieux de Memoire*." *Environment and Planning D: Society and Space* 23: 481-504.

Leitner, H., Jamie Peck, and E. S. Sheppard, eds. (2007). *Contesting Neoliberalism: Urban Frontiers*. New York, Guilford Press.

Lennon, J., and M. Foley. (2010). *Dark Tourism: The Attraction of Death and Disaster*. London, Thomson.

Lepawsky, J. (2005). "Stories of Space and Subjectivity in Planning the Multimedia Super Corridor." *Geoforum* 36(6): 705-719.

Leshkowich, A. M. (2012). "Rendering Infant Abandonment Technical and Moral: Expertise, Neoliberal Logics, and Class Differentiation in Ho Chi Minh City." *Positions: Asia Critique* 20(2): 497-526.

Leshkowich, A. M. (2011). "Making Class and Gender: (Market) Socailist Enframing of Traders in Ho Chi Minh City." *American Anthropologist* 113(2): 277-290.

Leshkowich, A. M. (2008). "Wandering Ghosts of Late Socialism: Conflict, Metaphor, and Memory in a Southern Vietnamese Marketplace." *Journal of Asian Studies* 67(1): 5-41.

Lloyd, K. (2004). "Tourism and Transitional Geographies: Mismatched Expectations of Tourism Investment in Vietnam." *Asia Pacific Viewpoint* 45(2): 197-215.

Luong, H. V., ed. (2009). *Urbanization, Migration, Poverty in a Vietnamese Metropolis: Ho Chi Minh City in Comparative Perspectives*. Singapore, National University of Singapore Press.

Luong, H. V., ed. (2003). *Postwar Vietnam: Dynamics of a Transforming Society*. Asian Voices. Singapore, Institute of Southeast Asian Studies and Rowman & Littlefield Publishers, Inc.

MacCannell, D. (1989). *The Tourist: A New Theory of the Leisure Class*. Berkeley, CA, University of California Press.

MacLean, K. (2012). "Enacting Anticorruption: The Reconfiguration of Audit Regimes in Contemporary Vietnam." *Positions: Asia Critique* 20(2): 595-625.

Malarney, S. K. (2011). Living with the War Dead in Contemporary Vietnam. *Everyday Life in Southeast Asia*. K. M. Adams and Kathleen A. Gillogly, eds. Bloomington, IN, Indiana University Press: 237-246.

Malesky, E., and J. London. (2014). "The Political Economy of Development in China and Vietnam." *Annual Review of Political Science* 17: 395-419.

McCann, E. (2013). "Policy Boosterism, Policy Mobilities, and the Extrospective City." *Urban Geography* 34(1): 5-29.

McCann, E. and K. Ward, eds. (2011). *Mobile Urbanism: Cities and Policymaking in the Global Age*. Minneapolis, MN, University of Minnesota Press.

McFarlane, C. (2011). "The City as a Machine for Learning." *Transactions of the Institute of British Geographers* 36(3): 360-376.

McGee, T. (2009). "Interrogating the Production of Urban Space in China and Vietnam Under Market Socialism." *Asia Pacific Viewpoint* 50(2): 228-246.

McHale, S. (2004). *Print and Power: Confucianism, Communism, and Buddhism in the Making of Modern Vietnam*. Honolulu, University of Hawaii Press.

Minca, C., and T. Oakes, eds. (2011). *Real Tourism*. London, Routledge.

Montoya, A. (2012). "From the 'People' to the 'Human': HIV/AIDS, Neoliberalism, and the Economy of Virtue in Contemporary Vietnam." *Positions: Asia Critique* 20(2): 561-591.

Muzaini, H. (2015). "On the Matter of Forgetting and 'Memory Returns.'" *Transactions of the Institute of British Geographers* 40(1): 102-112.

Muzaini, H. (2014). "The Afterlives of Memory Politics of the Ipoh Cenotaph in Perak, Malaysia." *Geoforum* 54: 142-150.

Muzaini, H., P. Teo, and B. Yeoh. (2007). "Intimations of Postmodernity in Dark Tourism: The Fate of History at Fort Siloso, Singapore." *Journal of Tourism and Cultural Change* 5(1): 28-45.

Muzaini, H., and B. S. A Yeoh. (2005). "War Landscapes as 'Battlefields' of Collective Memories: 'Reading' the Reflections at Bukit Chandu, Singapore." *Cultural Geographies* 12(3): 345-365.

Nguyen, P. A. (2006). "State-Society Relations in Contemporary Vietnam: An Examination of the Arena of Youth." *Asia Pacific Viewpoint* 47(3): 327-341.

Nguyen, V. T. (2012). "Refugee Memories and Asian American Critique." *Positions: Asia Critique* 20(3): 911-942.

Nguyen, T. A., J. Rigg, T. T. H., Luong, and T. D. Dinh. (2012). "Becoming and Being Urban in Hanoi: Rural-Urban Migration and Relations in Vietnam." *Journal of Peasant Studies* 39(5): 1103-1131.

Nguyen-Marshall, V., L. Drummond, and D. Bélanger, eds. (2012). *The Reinvention of Distinction: Modernity and the Middle Class in Urban Vietnam*. London, Springer.

Nguyễn-võ, T.-H. (2008). *The Ironies of Freedom: Sex, Culture, and Neoliberal Governance in Vietnam.* Seattle, University of Washington Press.

Nora, P. (1989). "Between Memory and History: Les Lieux de Memoire." *Representations* 26: 7-24.

Oakes, T. (2012). "Looking Out to Look In: The Use of the Periphery in China's Geopolitical Narratives." *Eurasian Geography and Economics* 53(3): 315-326.

Ormond, M. (2013). *Neoliberal Governance and International Medical Travel in Malaysia.* London, Routledge.

Pashigian, M. J. (2012). "Counting One's Way onto the Global Stage: Enumeration, Accountability, and Reproductive Success in Vietnam." *Positions: Asia Critique* 20(2): 529-558.

Peck, J., N. Theodore, and N. Brenner. (2010). "Postneoliberalism and its Malcontents." *Antipode* 41(s1): 94-116.

Peck-Barnes, S. (2000). *The War Cradle: Vietnam's Children of War: Operation Babylift— The Untold Story.* Denver, CO, Vintage Pressworks.

Pelley, P. (2002). *Postcolonial Vietnam: New Histories of the National Past.* Durham, NC, Duke University Press.

Peterson, P. (1981). *City Limits.* Chicago, University of Chicago Press.

Peycam, P. (2013). "From the Social to the Political: 1920s Colonial Saigon as a 'Space of Possibilities" in Vietnamese Consciousness.' *Positions: Asia Critique* 21(3): 497-546.

Peycam, P. (2012). *The Birth of Vietnamese Political Journalism: Saigon, 1916-1930.* New York, Columbia University Press.

Phong Lê. (1991). "Heading Toward a New Stage of Development of Culture, Literature and Art." *Tạp Chí Cộng Sản (Communist Journal)* JPRS-ATC-91-008: 16-18.

Raco, M., and K. Gilliam. (2012). "Geographies of Abstraction, Urban Entrepreneurialism, and the Production of New Cultural Spaces: The West Kowloon Cultural District, Hong Kong." *Environment and Planning A* 44(6): 1425-1442.

Reid-Henry, S. (2007). "The Contested Spaces of Cuban development: Post-Socialism, Post-Colonialism and the Geography of Transition." *Geoforum* 38(3): 445-455.

Rojek, C. and J. Urry, eds. (1997). *Touring Cultures: Transformations of Travel and Theory.* London, Routledge.

Sachs, D. (2011). *The Life We Were Given: Operation Babylift, International Adoption, and the Children of War in Vietnam.* New York, Beacon Press.

Salazar, N. B. (2010). *Envisioning Eden: Mobilizing Imaginaries in Tourism and Beyond.* New York, Berghahn.

Sasges, G., and S. Cheshier. (2012). "Competing Legacies: Rupture and Continuity in Vietnamese Political Economy." *South East Asia Research* 20(1): 5-33.

Savitch, H. and P. Kantor. (2004). *Cities in the International Marketplace.* Princeton, NJ, Princeton University Press.

Scheyvens, R. (2011). "The Challenge of Sustainable Tourism Development in the Maldives: Understanding the Social and Political Dimensions of Sustainability." *Asia Pacific Viewpoint* 52(2): 148-164.

Schumpeter, J. A. (1934). *Theory of Economic Development: An Inquiry into Profits, Capital, Credit, Interest and the Business.* Cambridge, MA, Harvard University Press.

Schwenkel, C. (2009). *The American War in Contemporary Vietnam: Transnational Remembrance and Representation.* Bloomington, Indiana University Press.

Schwenkel, C. (2006). "Recombinant History: Transnational Practices of Memory and Knowledge Production in Contemporary Vietnam." *Cultural Anthropology* 21(1): 3-30.

Schwenkel, C. (2014). "Rethinking Asian Mobilities: Socialist Migration and Post-Socialist Repatriation of Vietnamese Contract Workers in East Germany." *Critical Asian Studies* 46(2): 235-258.

Schwenkel, C., and A. M. Leshkowich. (2012). "Guest Editors' Introduction: How is Neoliberalism Good to Think Vietnam? How is Vietnam Good to Think Neoliberalism?" *Positions: Asia Critique* 20(2): 379-401.

Scott, S., F. Miller, and K. Lloyd. (2006). "Doing Fieldwork in Development Geography: Research Culture and Research Spaces in Vietnam." *Geographical Research* 44(1): 28-40.

Silverman, E. K. (2012). "From Cannibal Tours to Cargo Cult: On the Aftermath of Tourism in the Sepik River, Papua New Guinea." *Tourist Studies* 12(2): 109-130.

Singh, S., ed. (2009). *Domestic Tourism in Asia: Diversity and Divergence*. London, Earthscan.

Small, I. V. (2012). "Embodied Economies: Vietnamese Transnational Migration and Return Regimes." *Sojourn: Journal of Social Issues in Southeast Asia* 27(2): 234-259.

Smith, A., and A. Stenning. (2006). "Beyond Household Economies: Articulations and Spaces of Economic Practice in Post-Socialism." *Progress in Human Geography* 30(2): 190-213.

Sonmez, S. F. (1998). "Tourism, Terrorism, and Political Stability." *Annals of Tourism Research* 25(2): 416-456.

Springer, S. (2010). "Neoliberalism and Geography: Expansions, Variegations, Formations." *Geography Compass* 4(8): 1025-1038.

Springer, S. (2009a). "Culture of Violence or Violent Orientalism? Neoliberalisation and Imagining the 'Savage Other' in Post-Transitional Cambodia." *Transactions of the Institute of British Geographers* 34(3): 305-319.

Springer, S. (2009b). "Violence, Democracy, and the Neoliberal 'Order': The Contestation of Public Space in Posttransitional Cambodia." *Annals of the Association of American Geographers* 99(1): 138-162.

Su, X. (2015). "Urban Entrepreneurialism and the Commodification of Heritage in China." *Urban Studies* 52(15): 2874-2889.

Su, X. (2011). "Commodification and the Selling of Ethnic Music to Tourists." *Geoforum* 42(4): 496-505.

Suntikul, W., R. Butler, and D. Airey. (2010). "Implications of Political Change on National Park Operations: Doi Moi and Tourism to Vietnam's National Parks." *Journal of Ecotourism* 9(3): 201-218.

Suntikul, W., D. Airey, and R. Butler, (2008). "A Periodisation of the Development of Vietnam's Tourism Accommodation since the Open Door Policy." *Asia Pacific Journal of Tourism Research* 13(1): 67-80.

Tai, H.-T. H., and M. Sidel, eds. (2012). *State, Society and the Market in Contemporary Vietnam*. London, Routledge.

Tai, H.-T. H. (2001). Introduction: Situating Memory. *The Country of Memory: Remaking the Past in Late Socialist Vietnam*. H. H. Tai, ed. Berkeley, University of California Press: 1-17.

Tao, T. C. H., and G. Wall. (2009). "Tourism as a Sustainable Livelihood Strategy." *Tourism Management* 30(1): 90-98.

Taylor, K. (1983). *The Birth of Vietnam: Sino-Vietnamese Relations to the Tenth Century and the Origins of Vietnamese Nationhood*. Berkeley, University of California Press.

Taylor, N. A. (2001). Framing the National Spirit: Viewing and Reviewing Painting under the Revolution. *The Country of Memory: Remaking the Past in Late Socialist Vietnam*. H.-T. H. Tai, ed. Berkeley, University of California Press: 109-134.

Taylor, P. (2003). Digesting Reform: Opera and Cultural Identity in Ho Chi Minh City. *Consuming Urban Culture in Contemporary Vietnam*. L. Drummond and Mandy Thomas, eds. London, RoutledgeCurzon: 138-154.

Taylor, P. (2001). *Fragments of the Present: Searching for Modernity in Vietnam's South*. Honolulu, University of Hawaii Press.

Thomas, M. (2001). "Public spaces, public disgraces: crowds and the state in contemporary Vietnam." *Sojourn: Journal of Social Issues in Southeast Asia* 16(2): 306-330.

Tonnesson, S. (1991). *The Vietnamese Revolution of 1945: Roosevelt, Ho Chi Minh and De Gaulle in a World at War*. London, Sage.

Truitt, A. (2013). *Dreaming of Money in Ho Chi Minh City*. Seattle, University of Washington Press.

Truitt, A. (2012). "The Price of Integration: Measuring the Quality of Money in Postreform Vietnam." *Positions: Asia Critique* 20(2): 629-656.

Turner, S. (2012). "Making a living the Hmong way: an actor-oriented livelihoods approach to everyday politics and resistance in upland Vietnam." *Annals of the Association of American Geographers* 102(2): 403-422.

Urry, J. (2003). *Global Complexity.* Cambridge, Polity.

Vietnam National Administration of Tourism (VNAT) (2014). Tourism Statistics-2013. (available online at:*http://www.vietnamtourism.com/en/index.php/news/cat/20*), accessed October 27, 2014.

*Vietnam News Agency.* (2010). Party Leader Tells Nation of Future Challenges Ahead (28 June). Hanoi: Vietnam News (available online at:*http://vietnamnews.vnagency.com.vn/Politics-Laws/200966/Party-leader-tells-nation-of-future-challenges-ahead.html*, accessed October 25, 2014).

Voelkner, N. (2014). "Affective Economies in the Governance of Trafficking and Sex Work in Vietnam." *Global Society* 28(3): 375-390.

Winter, T. (2008). "Post-Conflict Heritage and Tourism in Cambodia: The Burden of Angkor." *International Journal of Heritage Studies* 14(6): 524-539.

Winter, T. (2007). "Rethinking Tourism in Asia." *Annals of Tourism Research* 34(1): 27-44.

Winter, T., Peggy Teo, and T. C. Chang, eds. (2009). *Asia on Tour: Exploring the Rise of the Asian Tourist.* London, Routledge.

Woodside, A. (1999). Exalting the Latecomer State: Intellectuals and the State during the Chinese and Vietnam Reforms. *Transforming Asian Socialism: China and Vietnam Compared.* A. Chan, B. Kerkvliet, and J. Unger, eds. London, Roman & Littlefield: 15-42.

Wu, F. (2002). "China's Changing Urban Governance in the Transition Towards a More Market-Oriented Economy." *Urban Studies* 39(7): 1071-1093.

Wu, F., and J. Zhang. (2007). "Planning the Competitive City-Region: The Emergence of Strategic Development Plan in China." *Urban Affairs Review* 42(5): 714-740.

Yeo, Y., and M. Painter. (2011). "Diffusion, Transmutation, and Regulatory Regime in Socialist Market Economies: Telecoms Reform in China and Vietnam." *The Pacific Review* 24(4): 375-395.

Yeung, H. W.-C. (2009). "Transnationalizing Entrepreneurship: A Critical Agenda for Economic Geography." *Progress in Human Geography* 33(2): 210-235.

Yúdice, G. (2003). *The Expediency of Culture.* Durham, NC, Duke University Press.

Zhang, L. (2012). "Afterword: Flexible Postsocialist Assemblages from the Margin." *Positions: Asia Critique* 20(2): 659-667.

Zimmerman, J. (2008). "From Brew Town to Cool Town: Neoliberalism and the Creative City Development Strategy in Milwaukee." *Cities* 25(4): 230-242.

Zukin, S. (2006). David Harvey on Cities. *David Harvey: A Critical Reader.* N. Castree and Derek Gregory, eds. London, Blackwell: 102-120.

# Index

Asia, 48–49
Asian Tiger. *See* Singapore
August Revolution, 35–36
Authority for the Protection and Safeguarding of the Angkor Region (APSARA), 97–98, 99

Ben Thanh market, 23
Ben Tre, 62, 64

Cambodia, 18, 96–99
China, 50, 53, 84, 96
command economy, 3, 48
commodification: of art, 45, 46; of memory, 67, 69–75, 76, 77, 78, 79; of tourist sites, 18, 52, 62, 63, 64, 68, 90, 93, 95
Communist Party of Vietnam. *See* state
Cu Chi Tunnels, 20, 27, 74, 92
cultural-economy, 2, 8, 9, 10, 13, 16, 19, 20, 28, 29, 31, 54, 74, 79, 85, 95, 96, 97, 99, 101, 102, 103; economic knowledge and, 24, 25; emblematic readings of, 27; evolution in, 26; moral values in, 23, 24, 100, 101, 102; passion in, 21, 22, 73; power in, 27; trust in, 25, 26, 51
culture: memory and, 68; as policy, 15, 31, 32, 33, 40, 48, 49; as resource, 11, 13, 33, 45, 48, 86, 95, 96, 97, 99; the sale of, 11, 20, 62, 63, 67, 74, 82, 89, 91
culture, national, 2, 6, 11, 16, 31, 32, 33, 35, 36, 37, 38, 39, 42, 43, 44, 46, 47, 48, 49, 74, 82, 84, 85, 86, 91, 93, 95, 97, 99, 101; arts and, 44, 45, 46; consumerism and, 41, 87, 88, 90; equitability and, 16, 40; "erosion of", 32, 34, 39, 40, 42, 85, 87; evolution of, 32; as material culture,

37; as oral tradition, 36; the reform era and, 39, 41, 94; resistance and, 16, 40; revolution and, 16, 33, 34, 35, 38, 40, 43, 45

đổi mới , *see* market reform

elderly, Vietnamese, 45
entrepreneurial city, Ho Chi Minh City as, 19–20, 27–28, 51–52, 54, 95; models of, 20, 21, 27, 64, 95, 100, 101
entrepreneurialism : critique of economic rationality in, 10, 20, 21, 24; extra-economic dimensions of, 2, 21, 27, 54, 102; model of governance and, 8, 9, 26, 27, 29, 51, 52, 54, 55; non-state forms of, 13, 17, 56, 64, 72, 77, 79, 89, 95, 97, 98, 99; the state's problems with, 5, 47, 48; state projections of, 2, 5, 15, 22, 27, 98, 100; tour guides and, 16, 17, 62, 63, 83; tourism actors' expediency over, 2, 11, 12, 13, 68, 69, 71, 74, 75, 76, 77, 79, 94, 95; urban, 52, 53, 56, 57, 58, 59, 60, 61
entrepreneurship. *See* entrepreneurialism

Gerald Ford, 71, 80n1
guides, tour, 20, 59, 62, 63, 64, 72, 73, 74, 81, 83, 90, 91, 92, 93

Hanoi, 7, 8, 21, 22, 33, 35, 39, 40, 43, 55, 57, 58, 80n2, 84, 90, 91
"Hanoi Hilton" (Hỏa Lò Prison), 41
Harvey, David, 8, 48, 49, 51, 52, 101
Ho Chi Minh City, 3, 6, 8, 16, 21, 26, 27, 51, 58, 91, 92, 93, 95, 96, 97; decentralization of, 19, 58; different historical periods of, 21, 26, 56;

# About the Author

**Jamie Gillen** is an assistant professor of geography at the National University of Singapore. His research centers on the cultural, urban, tourism, and political geographies of Vietnam. His new research projects include Vietnamese tourist encounters in the world and critiques of the Asian century.

Lightning Source UK Ltd.
Milton Keynes UK
UKOW02n1540200416

272648UK00001B/86/P